Distinctions

Richer Relationships *for* a More Satisfying Life

By
Shannon M. Mason, MSEd, PhD

27TH FLOOR PUBLICATIONS
TRENTON, NJ

Vital Distinctions
Richer Relationships for
a More Satisfying Life

By Shannon M. Mason, MSEd, PhD

ISBN: 978-0-9998942-0-0

Published by
27th Floor Publishing
Trenton, NJ

Cover Design: Eric Labacz, www.labaczdesign.com

For those who have most consistently and most convincingly loved me.
For my mother who taught me sacrifice and patience.
For my father who taught me courage and unapologetic truth.
For my sister who taught me acceptance and individuality.
For my brother who taught me to chase my dreams.
For my college girlfriends turned "sisters" who push me when I haven't gone far enough and pull me back when I've gone too far.
For my niece, the amazing young woman, to whom I want to leave a better world and for whom I will always be grateful.
For all the people who have allowed me to counsel them, encourage them, inquire of them, learn from them, pastor them, and simply sit with them in the ashes. And those who have done the same for me.
This is for you.

Why I Wrote This Book

In 15 years as a therapist and 13 years as pastor I have made one observation consistently: The quality of people's relationships determines the quality of their lives. People who seem to "have it all together" but lack healthy nourishing relationships often diminish. People who have tremendous financial, health or social challenges but enjoy healthy nourishing relationships thrive. I have also observed that people tend to struggle with the same things in relationships, and that success in other domains in life (i.e. academic and professional) does not insulate them from these struggles: boundaries, conflict, offense, and forgiveness, to name a few. I wrote this book because as I have spoken about these things in various settings (conferences, one-on-one conversations, counseling, small gatherings, etc.) people have found my thoughts to be tremendously helpful. I want to normalize these struggles, reduce shame, and provide practical perspective and guidance to pervasive relationship issues.

Table of Contents

Introduction

This Book Is for You!

We were vacationing in Myrtle Beach, South Carolina, when my niece fell in love with the boogie board. It provided for her both a sense of adventure and a boost in confidence. She ventured further and further out into the ocean until she hopped off her boogie board and found her feet no longer touched the bottom. Her screams were piercing, and as I ran out to her I was suddenly assaulted by my own thought, "I can't swim!" All I had were my long legs and my big mouth—so I ran out as far as I could and coached her in the rest of the way. In her panic, she had forgotten she actually *did* know how to swim.

As I held her shivering, panic-stricken body in my arms, neither of us had ever been so scared. "You can stay here in my arms for a little while longer," I said. "Then you have to go back into the ocean."

To her it seemed like a death sentence. She pleaded with me to reconsider. I refused. She looked to family members sitting nearby to reason with me. They refused. I sensed if this were her last memory of the ocean, she would never again enjoy it. All that she loved about it would forever be obscured by this one mishap.

I was reminded of the day I got into my first fender bender. I was seventeen, had just gotten my driver's permit…and could not believe I had actually just hit something! I threw my mother's evergreen Mercury Villager into "Park" and jumped out. Once safe on the sidewalk, and assured the damage was negligible, I proceeded to tearfully beg my mother to drive us the rest of the way home. She refused. She said, "If you stop driving now, you will never drive again." I didn't believe her at the time, but she was going to stand on the side of the freeway until I got back into the driver's seat, so I reluctantly climbed behind the wheel and have been driving ever since.

Just as my mother's wisdom and tough love saved driving for me, my wisdom and tough love were determined to save the ocean for my niece. Not fifteen minutes after her piercing screams signaled danger, she clenched my hand as we walked back toward the waves, trembling but together.

This book is written for those who at some point lost their footing and almost drowned in the sea of relationships. Perhaps it was a family relationship that became insufferable, friendship severed by betrayal, a business relationship that overpromised and underdelivered, or a romantic relationship that had a devastating and disorienting end. You may be in the initial stages of shock at the realization that footing has been lost, clawing your way back to the shore, or as you read these words, you may be shivering shoreside having decided you are simply "done." This book is for you. My hope is in these pages you will find a trustworthy hand to help guide you back into the ocean—trembling but together.

Chapter 1

It's All About the Nuances

In fifteen years of walking with others through relational minefields as a counseling psychologist and as a pastor, plus four decades of walking through my own, I found while most people who have been injured want be healed, the vast majority of them would much prefer to do so without the burden of a process. People want to be "fixed" quickly or "get over" what has happened to them and would much prefer the magic wand variety of fixing to the yellow brick road version. "Tell me what I need to do to get over this." "So will saying *that* bring an end to this?"

To be honest, I do not know if "getting over it" is the noblest goal. I think our relationships, and therefore our lives, become richer and more satisfying when, rather than "getting over it," we learn to live in light of our new realities. Pain is not a page to be ripped out of a book, leaving the other pages unaffected. If properly honored and employed, pain can be a master teacher giving value and clarity to the pages that follow. It must be worked through.

People who "just get over it" soon find themselves in equally, if not more harmful, situations and relationships. It is those who do the long hard work of "working through it" who truly heal. Working through it is a matter of examining, evaluating, learning from, and growing as a result of the pain. It is not escaping the pain of relational ruptures, but rather capitalizing on the pain associated with them. "Working through it" is all about the nuances.

To be clear, "working through it" does not necessarily mean professional counseling. I have seen faith communities, coaching, and even exercise provide the type of acceptance, perspective, courage, motivation, strategy, and reinforcement necessary to

It is those who do the long hard work of "working through it" who truly heal.

bring healing and produce lasting change, but only to the extent they help people catch the nuances. Nuances include the difference between a relationship that challenges and one that controls: strong and domineering, confident and arrogant, weak and meek, manipulative and afraid, detached and insecure. The nuances are obvious from the outside, and obvious to people after they have healed; that is why they say that "hindsight is 20/20." But nuances are not as obvious in the wake of injury. In the wake of injury, driving and crashing are the same, and ocean is synonymous with drowning.

Hence these distinctions. It is the little things that get lost when we are hurting, but also the little things that make a big difference in the quality of our relationships, and therefore in the quality of our lives. I offer these "vital distinctions" for those who do not want their pain to be their final page.

Chapter 2

What Did I Expect?

I grew up with the music of the 1950s and 1960s. We lived on the first floor of a two-family house. My maternal grandparents lived on the second floor, and theirs was the home where our entire extended family gathered. Almost weekly we'd all be together. Holidays went without saying. There were always lots of people, lots of food, and lots and lots of music.

My grandmother would drag me into the middle of the kitchen floor and make me jitterbug with her. I secretly loved it, but part of my preteen brain required me to feign disinterest. At two years old, my younger sister would run around the house singing Fats Domino's version of "Don't Mess With My Toot Toot." Occasionally the "young folks" favorites would get a spin on the record player, or on the full-size jukebox we had in our basement. To clarify, "the young folks" were not my me and my cousins. We were just "the kids," and by the time the oldest of us turned thirteen we would be firmly in the grip of the music video craze and ditch the old folks for MTV and BET. These "young folks" were actually our parents: the bridge generation. When they got to choose songs from the jukebox, kids, young folks, and grandparents alike might find ourselves belting out the lyrics to The Spinners' "Could It Be I'm Falling in Love" and "It Takes a Fool to Learn that Love Don't Love Nobody."

These gatherings were filled with love and laughter, and, of course, the occasional conflict—after all, we are family. In retrospect, the music that so beautifully articulated my grandparents' and parents' experiences with love also primed us. In a very palpable sense we were being taught love can be both the most beautiful of human experiences as well as the most painful.

Look at the lyrics to "Could It Be I'm Falling in Love," written by Melvin and Mervin Steals. That song was everything wonderful about love. Even sharp-tongued aunties and grumpy detached uncles would find a way back to each other for lingering moments during that song. It was mesmerizing. We kids didn't really know what they were dancing "about" *per se*, but we knew it was magnetic. We giggled as we, on one hand, needed to look on, and on the other hand, felt like intruders. They were in the middle of the kitchen floor with everybody else. This was the same kitchen where the grown-ups played cards and the grandmothers swapped recipes, the same kitchen where they would stop talking and start "spelling" out the most interesting words in their stories in order to protect our innocent ears from "grown-up conversation." ("Well, I heard that he didn't show up because he was in j-a-i-l."). This was the same kitchen where we got our hair washed and pressed, got calls from the hospital that left our worlds shattered (again), and even the same kitchen where we ate. But seeing our aunts and uncles rediscover each other to those songs made it sacred space. "Could it be I'm falling in love…with you….”

There were other songs, still about love—somehow the songs were almost *always* about love—but love of a different flavor. Songs like “It Takes a Fool,” also by The Spinners, left a different texture in the air with its refrain of “It takes a fool,” and “love don’t love nobody.”

It seems as though we received competing messages about love. From “And darling you'll always be the only one for me. Heaven made you specially” to “Love don’t love nobody” all on the same mixed tape—how could we expect to develop a healthy understanding of love? As experiences eventually teach us, that *is* the story of love. It is blissful—and painful. It is emboldening—and scary. It is breath-giving and breath-taking. Love has “iatrogenic effects.”

When natural and social scientists talk about iatrogenic effects, typically they refer to intrinsic and sometimes adverse effects resulting from a physician’s intervention or a therapy. These are elements necessary for the treatment, but also have their own distinct impact.

Cancer patients, for example, may undergo chemotherapy. The same treatment administered in order to destroy cancer cells may also destroy healthy cells. Among the many consequences are nausea, vomiting, and hair loss we have come to associate with “being on chemo.” The destruction of cancer cells is the goal of the treatment. The hair loss is an iatrogenic effect. If only we could have the treatment without the iatrogenic effect. The dead cancer cells without the sickness and hair loss. If only we could have the love without the pain. “It takes a fool to learn that love don’t love nobody.”

That is the characteristic of love The Spinners were honing in on. Love entails vulnerability. Vulnerability comes with the potential for pain. Certainly, we can have pain without vulnerability and love. But we cannot have love without vulnerability and at least the potential for pain.

The same aspect of chemo that heals you also hurts and destroys cells. The same aspect of love that heals you also hurts vulnerability. The good news is we can stop beating ourselves up for having been vulnerable. Vulnerability is an inescapable attribute of love.

Love is sacrificial and self-effacing. It requires giving. A lot. It requires caring. A lot. Love can be overwhelming. (Have you ever jumped out of bed in the middle of the night to make sure that your newborn was still breathing?) Love is risky, and costly,

Love is sacrificial and self-effacing.
It requires giving.

and has few absolute guarantees, and as such it sometimes involves "hurts." Thankfully, that is not the whole story of love, nor is it the best part. The best part is that we often forget in the wake of injury—love also heals. Practically speaking, love can protect us from burnout, help us cope with stressful situations, improve recovery from physical injury and illness, boost immune system functioning, decrease anxiety and depression, and make our brains healthier. Love's most significant work, its *magnum opus*, is it reconciles us back to our best selves. It reunites us to who we were before fear broke in.

Tragically, by seeking the benefits of love without its risk, many have forsaken genuine love in favor of artificial fillers. That in itself is a vital distinction: genuine love or artificial filler?

We long to create something meaningful, but find the vulnerability aspect of creativity too onerous. So we work too hard in jobs (or relationships) that are too small for us so we can point to something that says "my life matters."

We want something in our lives that speaks of our worth so we buy more stuff. Our closets, basements, and garages cannot conceal the cracks in our self-image. How can the emperor spend hundreds of dollars per month on a storage unit and still have no clothes?

We want company, but scoff at true companionship so we settle for serial frivolous "romantic" non-attachments. We wear these "situationships" and "friends with benefits" as costumes allowing us to dress up as "normal" and, for a few hours every now and then, we welcome the opportunity to forget what we fear—that we really are alone.

We want "love" without the vulnerability, and it just doesn't work.

Chapter 3

Love Is Therapy: It Helps Us Recover

In my doctoral research I was interested in understanding how people use religious faith to help them with substance abuse recovery. I became fascinated by this topic through a woman who had been attending the church I belonged to at the time. For many years she had been living on the streets and had been addicted to crack. Then one day she wasn't anymore. Literally, in a day she was no longer addicted to drugs. In the charismatic church world we refer to this phenomenon as "deliverance." I wanted to know if the field of counseling psychology knew about deliverance. What would they think of this? To be clear, I was not looking to use psychology to validate deliverance. Her deliverance was its own validation. I was honestly more curious about how my colleagues would clinically approach this situation if it showed up in their office.

Imagine:

"Dr. Walker, I know you have been treating me for substance dependence for a few months now. I have been in and out of treatment programs like this for years and, as I told you before,

I didn't really have much faith this one would work either. But yesterday I went to this church service and got delivered. I won't be back!"

I wanted to know more about the experiences of people who had been through deliverance, also known as "spontaneous recovery" in the clinical world. I wanted to understand the elements and whether there were similarities between their experiences and the experiences of those who go through more of a process over time. As it often happens with dissertation research, my topic continued to morph until I ultimately ended up interviewing people who saw their faith as a significant factor in their recovery—whether spontaneously recovered or recovered through a process over time.

With permission I recorded interviews and spent months and months poring over these transcripts to identify significant

Love helps to create and recreate the conditions conducive to recovery of our original intention and purpose.

themes. I was most interested in the themes that were repeated across the interviews, although some unique themes also helped shaped my thinking. At the center of it all I was delighted to find love.

Each participant shared how critical the love received from a "concerned other" in their faith community was in their recovery process. For some, the "concerned other" was God. For others, the "concerned other" was an individual who they connected with in a local church. In either case, study participants universally reported that this love, accompanied by the acceptance, care, encouragement, and role-modeling they received, had significant bearing on their recovery process. Whether they went through a six-month program, or a six-minute spiritual experience, love was at the center of it their recovery process.

Here are a few quotes from the people I interviewed.

"In the church [there was] compassion. These people [didn't] get paid to do what they did, you know. The stuff they were doing for me...it was because it was in their heart. I could feel that in their heart they truly, truly were compassionate and worried about my life.... They looked at me like a prize...I don't remember ever being looked at the way they looked at me."

–JN

"Jesus. I was missing God. Missing that through His love and His mercy [He] showed me that I was worth something, and when I realized that I was worth something, I started to complete things."

–KP

"What helped me at that point...this is one of the greatest things that I think really helped me, was that she reached out to me. She didn't reach out to me and try to force religion on me. She just reached out to me in little simple ways.... It was a great experience being around her all the time. She really kept me in her wings. I mean she really kept me [under] her wings, and then some good things started to happen for me."

–CW

"Show them that they're worthy and that God has already

forgiven them. That they're somebody...So we have to show them that this thing can be done out of love..."

–KP

When I say "love is therapy" I do not mean to imply love is a worthwhile addition to our lives simply because it helps to fix broken stuff. Rather, like any truly affective therapy, love helps to create and recreate the conditions conducive to recovery of our original intention and purpose. The writer of the epistle of John said it best:

"We know how much God loves us, and we have put our trust in His love. God is love, and all who live in love live in God, and God lives in them. And as we live in God our love grows more perfect."

1 John 4:16-17

Chapter 4

Love Is the End

The epistle, or letter, of John was written to a group of people who made the substantial investment of their lives in a relationship and were wondering "is it worth it?" After all, in exchange for their commitment and considerable personal sacrifice they were suffering harassment, intimidation, disappointment, and loss. They had such high hopes for life in this path called "The Way," but the journey had been far more treacherous than they thought. They had concerns, some may have even had regrets. Yet through the noise of uncertainty the writer offers a single measuring stick, one criterion to help them evaluate their past decisions, investments, and sacrifices. One indicator of whether and how they should move forward. One touchstone from which they can come to terms with the unanticipated parts of their stories. The writer offers one beautifully elegant standard: love. The goal, he says, is to love, continue loving, and just keep getting better at loving.

"We know how much God loves us, and we have put our

> *trust in His love. God is love, and all who live in love live in God, and God lives in them. And as we live in God, our love grows more perfect. So we will not be afraid on the day of judgment, but we can face Him with confidence because we live like Jesus here in this world."*
>
> 1 John 4:16-17

The implications are tremendous! By growing in love we become better than our best selves, we become more like God! By growing in love we are reclaiming our lives from fear. Here is the most startling of all the implications: Even if things have not turned out as I anticipated, if I loved I won.

When relationships fail we ask ourselves a lot of questions.

- Was I too_____?
- Should I have____?
- What would have happened if only_____?

But if love does all that the apostle John and my research participants suggest, perhaps the most relevant question is "Did I love?"

That helps me! That helps me...A LOT!

I can identify with this first audience. Can you? Haven't we all committed and made substantial relational investments only to be left wondering whether or not it was worth it? We love people who end up betraying or abandoning us. We love people and discover they were not in it for the same reasons we were. We wonder if they ever really loved us at all, and then become angry with ourselves because a part of us still loves them. Love often doesn't turn out the way we expect it to. Loved ones up and die on us, spouses betray, co-workers get laid off, and friends abandon. We are left ripped apart.

Why even bother risking such loss? Does it really take a fool to learn that "love don't love nobody?"

We risk love because, despite our cultural suspicions and personal ambiguities about love, love is still worthwhile. Love is good for us, not because we can use it as leverage or collateral to get something else that is better for us. Love is good for us because love is good for us. Love is its own reward.

In his memoir recounting his harrowing experience in Nazi death camps during World War II, Viktor Frankl describes unimaginable suffering. The indignities of starvation, infestation, brutality, and squalor overtake him. The unrelenting presence of death and survival obsession leads to a kind of separation of himself from himself.

> *"When the last layers of subcutaneous fat had vanished, and we looked like skeletons disguised with skin and rags, we could watch our bodies beginning to devour themselves, ..."*
>
> -excerpts from Viktor Frankl *Man's Search for Meaning*

It is hard to imagine where one might find beauty and satisfaction among these scenes, but Frankl does!

> *"A thought transfixed me: for the first time in my life I saw the truth as it is set into song by so many poets, proclaimed as the final wisdom by so many thinkers. The truth—that love is the ultimate and highest goal to which man can aspire."*

Love God...Love Others

There are 613 laws comprising the Mosaic law. Six hundred and thirteen laws! Some of them, such as "you shall not commit murder," are widely regarded and accepted as necessary foundations for a "civilized" society. Others such as "remember the Sabbath and keep it holy," though countercultural, are definitely admirable. One entire day of no work, not even checking emails. Admirable, right?

Then there are those who seem, to the modern mind, confusing and honestly a bit weird, such as dietary regulations that only permit eating animals that have split hooves *and* chew the cud. Never mind the prohibition on mixing meat and dairy (no cheeseburgers). Then there are 610 more of them!

So when a crafty religious leader asked Jesus to "bottom-line it for me," I can imagine the crowd falling dead silent as they waited with bated breath to see what He would say in response to *that!* Could there be a common thread that invisibly yet powerfully held together ideas as divergent as how to deal with interpersonal injustice, worship of the Creator, sexual ethics, care for the poor and the stranger, contain communicable disease, and what to eat for dinner? Jesus lays it on them. "Love the Lord your God and your neighbor as yourself." Bottom line: love. Period.

Love is the principle thing

Again Frankl's words strike a chord,

> *"We who lived in concentration camps can remember the men who walked through the huts comforting others, giving away their last piece of bread. They may have been few in number, but they offer sufficient proof that everything can*

be taken from a man but one thing: the last of the human freedoms—to choose one's attitude in any given set of circumstances, to choose one's way."

My hope is we will all again choose the way of love. *"For love is as strong as death, its jealousy as enduring as the grave. Love flashes like fire, the brightest kind of flame."*

Song of Solomon 8:6 NLT

"If I speak with human eloquence and angelic ecstasy but don't love, I'm nothing but the creaking of a rusty gate. If I speak God's Word with power, revealing all his mysteries and making everything plain as day, and if I have faith that says to a mountain, 'Jump,' and it jumps, but I don't love, I'm nothing.

If I give everything I own to the poor and even go to the stake to be burned as a martyr, but I don't love, I've gotten nowhere. So, no matter what I say, what I believe, and what I do, I'm bankrupt without love."

1 Corinthians 12:1-3

Chapter 5

Be Good to Yourself

My college mailbox was usually jam-packed with event flyers, credit card offers, and the dreaded pink envelope, which housed my campus phone bill. I still carefully waded through the pile because "Grandma Mason" loved writing letters...and I loved receiving letters from her. The sight of that Okahumpka, Florida, return address in impeccable cursive handwriting made my heart flutter. Then there was the guilt. "Did I write her back the last time? Did I even call to say I had received her letter?" What I would give to receive one of those letters again.

Whether a brief check-in or a lengthy update on the family, her church, the state of everyone's health, and her hopes for the next holiday gathering, all of Grandma's letters ended the same: "Be good to yourself." I wonder if she was trying to remind her highly driven, results-oriented eldest granddaughter, who often reached the goal but missed the point, that her ability to do good and be good to the world was not divorced from her ability to do good and be good to herself. It could never be an either/or. It would always be a both/and. Love yourself and then you can approach the world with a sense of moral proportion.

What does it look like to love oneself? At the time that I was receiving those letters in my college mailbox it probably looked like eating the pizza *and* the ice cream for dinner. Decades later it looks like dragging myself out of bed to work out because this cholesterol is not going to lower itself. Intangible love is discerned by tangible behaviors. This is why many of us experience such dissonance with regard to relationships. We have been told we were "loved" by people who promptly proceeded to treat us badly. They "loved" us but abandoned us, or "loved" us but abused us, or "loved" us but were unfaithful to us. Their words and behaviors are at best in tension with one another and at worst in conflict. We are left with a vicious dilemma. We must either throw away our definition of love in order to preserve the relationship, or throw away the relationship in order to preserve our definition of love. It's the dissonance that destroys.

What does love look like when it takes on hands and feet and walks into the kitchen? How is it discernible? In *All About Love,* author bell hooks posits love is the mixing of various ingredients. Among them are care, affection, recognition, respect, commitment, trust, and honest and open communication. So when my grandmother was cultivating my burgeoning self-love in the close of each of her letters, she was saying care for yourself, be affectionate towards yourself, recognize yourself, respect yourself, be committed to yourself, trust yourself, be honest with yourself, and be open to yourself. These are the evidences of love, and when these evidences are well-practiced at home, they are easily recognizable in the world. "Be good to yourself" and you will know what "love" sounds like, acts like, and looks like in the world.

The truth is the well-loved have advantages in this world. They tend to balance generosity and selectivity well, giving much of themselves to others, but the best of themselves to few. They tend to be less tolerant of maltreatment of themselves and others, and not easily seduced by empty flattery. They are clearer about what they want, what they must have and what they absolutely cannot tolerate in themselves and others, and they seem to attract the resources needed to get it. They can take responsibility readily and apologize quickly. They know what it is like to be scandalously naked yet unashamed. Love is the superfood of the soul.

> *Be good to yourself and you will know what "love" sounds like, acts like, and looks like in the world.*

Then there are the others—those who spend their lives wondering if they are loveable. They fear inadequacy. They equate vulnerability with weakness. They hide rather than own up to personal limitations. They waste energy and goodwill trying to craft others into a more acceptable image, because that is what they assume others are always doing to them. They spend life hiding—not because they don't want to be seen but because they dread what there is to see.

The truth is both the well-loved and the wonderers will stumble through life at times feeling as if they have gotten love wrong. That is not the tragedy. The tragedy is to stop stumbling. Paralyzed by the fear of love gone wrong, many cease to try.

In *The Book of Joy*, His Holiness the Dalai Lama and Archbishop Desmond Tutu warns of the "fashionable cynicism that risks engulfing us." It is truth. Cynicism is popular, particularly cynicism about love, and for good cause. Life is hard. Love is risky. Armor is desirable. Cynicism is good armor. The problem, however, is cynicism doesn't just *protect* us from the dangers of love, it *prevents* us from experiencing love altogether. It is the risks involved that makes love so rewarding. We are compelled to risk loving ourselves, then to risk loving others. I started off with the notion it is the distinctions or nuances that can get lost in our relational pain. It is also the nuances that must be recovered in order to love well and live well. I've tried arguing on love's behalf, as I realize some people doubt. Now we turn to those distinctions that help us become better than our best selves (like GOD!) as we grow in love. That is the ultimate goal—growing in love so that pain is not our final page.

Chapter 6

Is It Love or Is It Lust?

I woke up one Friday morning and found myself unable to walk. My legs worked fine but I couldn't get oriented. Dizzy does not even begin to describe what I was experiencing.

A couple of hours later I almost laughed when the emergency room doctor told me I had a brain tumor. It was a combination of nervous disbelief and the desire to lighten the announcement, which had reached my best friend's ears the same moment it reached mine, that left me wanting to giggle. That sensation was immediately quenched when he handed me the image from my MRI. I have studied the brain, so I was confused by my own confusion as I looked at the image and could not identify the tumor. Furthermore, I couldn't remember what the big thing in the middle of my brain was called. *It's not the frontal lobe. It's not the parietal lobe. It's close to but not actually the occipital lobe,* I thought, before the unwelcomed interruption. "THAT'S the tumor," he said. "It's huge!" was all I could blurt out before my attention needed to be diverted to fighting back the tears. "It has been growing for years," he said. "Didn't you have any symptoms?"

"Well, there were headaches. But, do normal people assume headaches mean a massive brain tumor?" I replied.

I thought I was tired. I thought I was stressed. I thought I needed another vacation, or a new job. I found lots of ways to explain away the pain, but the truth is having that huge tumor hogging up my brain space hurt!

It hurt to have a "pituitary macroadenoma." It hurt even more to have it surgically removed—through my nose no less! It hurt when the ear, nose, and throat specialist went up there to check the incision was healing properly. Even after it healed, it still hurt. At inexplicable times the pain would re-emerge like a plastic ball breaking free from a child determined to bury it in the pool—splashing everything around it and creating a mess. This hurt lasted for what seemed to me an utterly unreasonably long time.

Discovering you are in love with someone who is in lust with you is kind of like that, a slow, insidious, suffocating, vision blurring, messy, splashing-on-everything type of hurt. It hurts to be in it and not realize. It hurts to finally realize what it is. It hurts to get out of it. It hurts to deal with it. It hurts to heal from it. Even after you think you are healed, the hurt pops up again, almost as powerfully as before. It hurts for what feels like an utterly unreasonably long time.

> *There are few things more toxic to the human soul than to be in love with someone who is in lust with you.*

I believe that there are few things more toxic to the human

soul than to be in love with someone who is in lust with you, and I suspect this is one of the reasons why many have come to the conclusion that "love don't love nobody." Love and lust have gotten confused, sometimes within the same person, and sometimes between different people within the same relationship.

Sometimes the love-lust dynamic has a pseudo-presence, meaning it may not be verifiably present, but since it has a cognitive and emotional presence, it functions as truth. "Did she ever really love me? If she ever really loved me, there is no way that she would have been able to do *that!"*

This, of course, is the perspective of the one who has loved and lost as opposed to the one who has lusted and lost. Most have been on both sides. Few are willing to admit it.

The man who has worked for a company for thirty years only to be unceremoniously dismissed due to "reorganization," the woman who has lost a close friendship over something seemingly trivial OR for reasons not articulated at all, the family member who is suddenly cold-shouldered because he or she is unable to provide yet another financial bail-out, the pastor who has invested significantly in an individual or an entire congregation only to be abandoned or replaced, share a common pain. Whether an actual presence or a pseudo-presence, the love-lust dynamic is there. One party had a different idea about the nature of the relationship than the other.

How Did We Get Here?

In almost any type of relationship we can find ourselves deeply connected to someone who is more attracted to the idea of us than the reality of us. It can be tricky, especially when we consider even genuine love relationships start off resembling lust. We encounter a stranger and see in them something we want for ourselves. It could be a physical feature we find desirable, but it could also be power, or status, or their intellect, or their general disposition we are drawn to. We approach the person in order to see if things are really as they appear, and ultimately to get access to what they have that we want. We start out lusting.

The difference is a healthy relationship grows from there. Based on the little bit we know and desire, we decide to give someone access to our lives. That access is limited at first—maybe it is just an email address (because if they turn out to be crazy we can always "spam" them), then a phone number, then phone time, face-to-face time, time with your friends and family, and so on. We commit to discovering them and allowing them to discover us and in the initial stages, we constantly reassess that commitment. As we get to know them we may grow in respect,

Deep anguish often resides at the intersection of love and lust.

admiration, and trust, and we may even find ourselves becoming an even better version of us because of their influence.

Of course, there is another option. We may commit to the discovery process only to learn things about them that undermines our respect or trust. Perhaps he consistently overpromises and underdelivers, or she chronically overspends. Maybe he curses at the dog, or disrespects his parents or lies, or has friends of questionable character—or no friends at all. Maybe she doesn't care about the poor, or the environment, or the sick, or anyone other than herself. From there we may decide we cannot continue in the relationship.

Friendships end, professional relationships dissolve, and family relationships splinter much for the same reasons romantic relationships end—lack of integrity, disloyalty, ineffective communication and/or neglect.

The point, though, is non-familial relationships start out because we admire something in someone and desire it for ourselves. The difference between love and lust is love broadens in its appreciation of the other. Lust remains in the "what's in this for me" mode.

Chapter 7

The Posture of Love

While still a broke graduate student, I was visiting the home of an older couple I admired. They were always impeccably dressed. Once I got to know them I discovered they were also always impeccably kind. I was excited about seeing their home. *If their clothing and cars are any indication,* I thought, *this is going to be good.* And good it was. What impressed me most that day was not the fine furnishings and interior design, but the artwork hanging in their family room. The perfectly coordinated frames caught my attention. As I walked across the room for a closer look, I was at first confused and then utterly delighted. These works of art were not masterpieces obtained from a fine art gallery. They were the scribbles of their toddler granddaughter. Love is like that. Love frames scribbles.

Deep anguish often resides at the intersection of love and lust. Sometimes people's early experiences have poorly trained them to recognize the differences between the two. They falsely believe that their love-worthiness is based on their ability to perform certain desirable tasks. They falsely associate love with pain—which makes sense especially if the first love object lessons made the same mistake. They believe the best way to get over love loss is to find a new person to pick up where things left off with the old person. They hide, diminish, and suffocate aspects of themselves in order to be more palatable to the person whose love they crave. They expect all of the goodness toward oneself to come from the outside world. They associate love with control, assimilation, pain, and make no distinction between passion and rage. I think at their core they know it is not love, but they fear this is all there really is because this is all they really have so they settle for it. They lack the knowledge of self to warn them when their self is being violated.

As a result they believe they are worthy of love based on certain performance indicators and end up connected to people who are more interested in the performance than the performer. Love is not like that.

Love is patient and kind. Love is not jealous or boastful or proud or rude. It does not demand its own way. It is not irritable, and it keeps no record of being wronged. It does not rejoice about injustice but rejoices whenever the truth wins out. Love never gives up, never loses faith, is always hopeful, and endures through every circumstance. Three things will last forever—faith, hope, and love—and the greatest of these is love.

1 Corinthians 13: 4-7, 13

Vital Distinctions: Love vs. Lust

Love is patient. Patience is generally associated with waiting, and some have said that patience is not *that* one waits but rather *how* one waits. And aren't relationships full of waiting? There is the waiting for the other to finish getting dressed so the dinner reservation won't be missed. Truthfully, that is the "easy" waiting. Think about the parents waiting for their child to finally catch on to potty training so she can go to preschool. What about the fiancé waiting for his intended to finish graduate school before getting married? What about waiting for another job offer after a financially devastating layoff? Waiting for him to return after a deployment? Waiting for her to retire before taking their dream vacation? What about waiting for him to catch up to what

Lust's opportunism and charm work well together to expose it for what it is.

you have been saying for the past six months?

Love seeks to understand other people, and then love works to respond to them based on that understanding. While it seems patience comes more easily to some people, I believe we can all learn to be more patient. Ultimately, love is willing to wait because it considers and values the whole of the person more than what is desired but delayed.

Lust, on the other hand, is opportunistic. Because lust is primarily self-motivated, lust looks like love until sacrifice is required. Lust will use the threat of abandonment to impose its will. Rarely is it willing to wait, and if it does, it punishes while waiting.

The next vital distinction is an important one—one easy to miss. **Love is kind, but lust is charming.** To the untrained eye, kindness and charm may look similar, but they have vastly different motivations. Kindness is intended to affirm the worth of another—to build others up. Period. Be impressed by hungry people who still manage to be kind to the waiter who messed up their order more than once. It means they may have a position of heart, seeking to see the value in people no matter the circumstance. Charm, on the other hand, is intended to arouse admiration in order to set the stage for exploitation. Charm tends to pour on rather heavily and can seem "too good to be true," unlike kindness, which seems to flow naturally from people who are well…kind. Kindness affirms, charm exploits. Charm often comes with demands and entitlements—the "you owe me" always shows up. I am amazed by how often women in abusive relationships report "he was so charming at first." Word to the wise, while kindness is pretty hard to fake, "charm is deceitful." Proverbs 31:30.

Lust's opportunism and charm work well together to expose it for what it is. When people are operating in lust, because their goal is to have their own way, they can be very charming while scouting for opportunity. The moment lust is thwarted, however, the fangs come out and they are revealed for who they really are. Some of the wisest relationship advice I ever received was "When someone shows you who they are, believe them."

The Practice of Love

Love is not jealous or boastful or proud or envious. Love puts other first, lust puts self first. Many years ago while attending a conference I heard a speaker say, "I can't be jealous of someone if I am praying for their success." These words set me free. At the time I was really struggling with feeling behind in life. Now I honestly don't remember which of my friends I thought was so far ahead of me, what they had that I wanted, or thought I deserved (and she didn't?). However, I do remember I was face-burning, shallow-breathing, jaw-clenching, eyes-rolling jealous. His words were the arrows that pierced my heart and flooded my eyes with tears.

Love wants others to do well, *especially* those closest to us. It is invested in the success of teammates. I started praying for my friend's success then and there, and my jealousy was replaced by gratitude for what was happening in her life.

Love seeks the highest good of another because it puts the other first, it is not jealous. Who has ever seen a cheerleader upset because his team is winning? Love does not try to one-up the success of the other—it is not boastful.

Have you ever had a friend or colleague who *always* had a story to top your story or a need to bring up an accomplishment to top your accomplishment? A former friend of mine would actually truncate my stories with, "That's nothing," before telling his "better" story. That compared with a lifelong friend who even if I needed to lose thirty pounds, celebrated my 1.5-pound loss as if I had just negotiated a deal securing world peace. Love frames scribbles.

Love is not proud or rude. I recently discovered an HGTV television show called "Love It or List It." The basic premise is a couple whose home is no longer functional for them seeks the aid of an interior designer and realtor who will respectively redesign their home and find them another with all the features they want. The husband and wife are always divided on whether they should try to stay in their current home, with one insisting they must stay, and the other insisting they must leave. The dynamic unfolding between the couple as they are presented with various options, disappointments, and setbacks is at least as exciting as the house hunting and renovation project portion of the show.

Of course, some, if not most, of the interactions are staged. It is after all a television show. I suspect at least some of it is not. What about the woman who throws a tantrum every time she cannot get her way and ends up $60,000 over budget as her husband gives in to her tantrums. I can't help but wonder, "What is the *real* cost of that $60,000 overrun?" Is it worth it to have one's way when it requires trampling on the sense of security of someone we claim to love?

Love is more concerned about what works for "us" than what works for me. Because it is more concerned about the success of the team, it is willing to take a momentary individual loss for a long-term team gain. Lust demands its own way screaming, "I am the most important thing." Love is willing to concede whispering, "We are the most important thing."

Love is not irritable, lust is. There is a shallowness to lust, and just like the sign at the pool warns, danger can result from diving in. We become irritated when we are being asked for more than we are willing to give. When lust is in operation, there is a low emotional and spiritual reservoir. The relationship may be able to handle endless receiving, but not very much giving. Can you see the danger yet? Exactly how much injury can result from a relationship in which both parties are only receivers? How about one in which one party is the designated giver and the other party is the designated receiver?

Love keeps no record of wrong.

Love does not mean amnesia. I do not believe we "forgive and forget" as much as we "forgive and create new and better memories." Love means paying diligent attention to the record of right, until the record of wrong begins to diminish.

One of my favorite undergraduate psychology professors taught me about "long-term potentiation." In short, long-term potentiation is the process whereby neural pathways become more efficient and connections become longer lasting. As communications between neurons are repeated, they start to communicate more quickly and their connections become stronger. For example, getting behind the wheel of a car for the first time, a teenager may have to methodically work through a mental checklist (seatbelt, key in ignition, turn the key, step on the brake, shift into D for drive, check surroundings, etc.). The longer a person has been

Love means paying diligent attention to the record of right, until the record of wrong begins to diminish.

driving, the less attention has to be paid to the each discrete step. It all flows together in a rhythm that feels automatic. After making the same connections over and over again, the connections become more efficient and stronger.

Another good illustration of long-term potentiation is walking across grass. I grew up in the city, and we didn't have as much reverence for grass as people in the suburbs did—at least as teenagers. Grass surrounding corner properties was particularly disrespected because the absence of a fence was an open invitation to cut through the grass in order to get to the store more quickly. I don't remember ever getting to the corner store and being disappointed they had run out of "quarter juices," Jingles, or Now and Laters (pronounced "naahnlaters"), but we were always looking for a shortcut so we made one, right across someone's front lawn.

One person cutting through the grass one day did not cause too much of a problem, except by cutting through the grass they made an alternative for others. Once it was established across the grass was an acceptable route, others followed suit day after day. Before long the beautifully growing lush green grass gave way to dirt, rocks, and even the wrappers from our treasured purchases. Long-term potentiation.

Love keeps no record of wrong in that it resists the easy and shorter pathways of blaming, guilting, shaming, and punishing—self and/or others. Love understands the short path destroys what

Love keeps no record of wrong in that it resists the easy and shorter pathways of blaming, guilting, shaming, and punishing—self and/or others.

is healthy and growing, causing relational vitality to give way to dirt, rocks, and debris. Love doesn't rehearse the wrong because such rehearsal destroys. It acknowledges the wrong, evaluates its impact, takes appropriate responsibility, develops a corrective action plan, implements the plan, celebrates successes, and then walks the longer, but life-sustaining, path of rehearsing the good.

Love keeps no record of wrong. Lust, on the other hand, hoards wrongs. Remember lust is in it to win it. Lust is always looking for leverage—a way to make sure that "I get what I deserve" or "I get what I want." To the lustful, wrongs suffered are currency. They can be used to shame and guilt others into compliance. Love is a treasure hunter, lust is a fault-finder.

Love does not rejoice about injustice but rejoices whenever truth wins out. Love is concerned about the means as well as the ends. It deliberates the potential consequences of words and actions and settles on doing what is right as opposed to doing what is simply expedient. Furthermore, love does not find the missteps, mishaps, and misfortunes of others entertaining. Love does not bolster one's own standing by degrading others.

Lust considers means irrelevant as long as the desired end is obtained.

Perhaps by now you are making mental notes about a current or previous relationship and are having some misgivings. The notes may be warranted, however, while this may sound like a checklist or a formula, in reality we are always working balance these tensions. In the healthiest love relationships, competing needs, and desires have to be managed. Sometimes being patient feels like being taken for granted, and the one that understands others feels least understood. Sometimes the dance between forgiveness and reconciliation is clumsy and inelegant. But love does not give up.

Love never gives up, never loses faith, is always hopeful, and endures through every circumstance. Love does not stop believing in the best in people and does not take failures as final.

It shuns the filtered and airbrushed images on which lust thrives, preferring and treasuring the beauty that includes scars.

"I still panic sometimes, forget to breathe, but I know that there's something beautiful in my imperfections; the beauty that he held up for me to see."

Crazy/Beautiful, 2001

More than twenty years ago, I heard a man talking about his

wife whom he had been visiting for the previous four years in a nursing home. He fed her lunch daily, and although they had been married for over two decades, she did not know who he was. She had Alzheimer's disease, yet he did not give up. He kept showing up, kept caring, kept serving, and kept clinging to his covenant even through what became a horrific ordeal. He loved her.

Chapter 8

When Loving You Is Killing Me

Besides being confused with lust, there are other ways that "love don't love nobody." Love does involve the giving of oneself to another. But which parts? How much? For how long? Under what conditions?

Among the most vital work of adult life is learning to immerse oneself in the life of another without losing one's own distinction. Boundaries help us to safely navigate that. Just as lane boundary lines on a highway or a fence around a yard limit access in order to improve safety, healthy emotional boundaries allow us to experience intimacy with others without losing ourselves. When they are violated, our response is often visceral. Shallow breathing, chest tightening, headaches, stomach aches, and digestive issues—our very bodies tell us we are not safe.

Many ignore these soul sirens, adjusting our boundaries for the sake of "peace" or the happiness of another. Both reflect an ill-conceived notion of love. We want to save the relationship. We want to save the other person. We want to prove our worth. Boundary adjustment is a losing strategy, because in doing so we establish a new and painful norm. We have also sometimes been taught that we are willing to sacrifice our wholeness in order to accommodate the brokenness of another. This is the very definition of a toxic relationship. It's really quite simple: Healthy people have a healthy respect for boundaries—both their own and those of others.

Consider the following story:

Dante was an up-and-coming professional. He was a hard worker, creative, intelligent, charismatic, funny, and everyone loved him. When he was recruited to work for one of the largest financial firms in the country, his family was elated. The CEO quickly took notice of him, and within months he was being assigned increasingly significant roles on projects. Before long, Dante became Mr. Jenson's "right-hand man." This only made Dante more popular among his colleagues, as it seemed Dante's presence had a calming effective on "the cranky old man," as Mr. Jenson's staff affectionately referred to him.

With Jenson delegating so much of his work to Dante, other people in the company started seeing Dante as the go-to guy as well. They would ask him to sit in on meetings, make special requests for him to review their presentations, or consult on aspects of their projects. It seemed Dante couldn't miss. When the quarterly earnings reports came out, the email congratulated "Jenson and his team" on an excellent quarter, but the word around the office was the success of the quarter was primarily due to Dante's efforts—and that became a problem.

As the rumor mill started working overtime, so did Jenson's paranoia. Jenson cancelled his car service and started having Dante pick him up for work every day. "That way we can be more efficient," he reasoned. Soon, Dante was picking up coffee, breakfast, and even dry cleaning on his way to pick up Jenson to drive him to work. Dante was initially flattered, but as workdays began extending further and further into the evening, and proof-reading turned to drafting turned to researching and drafting turned to doing everything except presenting, the flattery dissipated. The final straw was when Dante took four weeks perfecting a big client presentation Jenson not only presented as his own, but also made disparaging and untruthful remarks about Dante after the presentation. After overhearing his mentor tell these clients that he had taken Dante under his wing in an attempt to help him after an "ethical dilemma" resulted in him being let go from his previous firm, Dante had enough. He submitted his resignation the next day.

Healthy emotional boundaries allow us to experience intimacy with others without losing ourselves.

Hopefully, the reader saw the slippery slope sooner than Dante did. It is, of course, much easier to recognize with hindsight than when we are the Dante in the story and Jenson is our boss, our romantic partner, our family member, or our friend.

Vital Distinction: Net vs. Noose

By definition a net is "a bag or other contrivance of strong thread or cord worked into an open meshed fabric, for catching fish, birds, or other animals." Its defining function is goal-directed support.

By definition a noose is "a loop with a running knot, tightening as the rope or wire is pulled and typically used to hang people or trap animals." It's defining function is entrapment.

There are some clear similarities between a net and a noose. Under certain conditions a net can even become a noose. Rarely is the reverse true. Both net and noose conjure images of a strong, fibrous material, interrelated in a way that allows each of them to bear significant weight. A noose, however, doesn't understand boundaries.

Boundaries keep us safe. Whether physical, emotional, or spiritual, they are in place for good reason. We need to be able to differentiate between our needs and the needs of others—and to honor that difference. When this is navigated well we become limit-setting, limit-respecting, generous, loving people who enjoy the freedom and intimacy of close relationships. That's the net. When this is not, the outcome is limit-resisting, resentful, anxious people whose relationships are full of bitterness and a sense of impending doom. That's the noose.

We need to be able to differentiate between our needs and the needs of others—and to honor that difference.

This noose experience is what Drs. Henry Cloud and John Townsend refer to as "boundary conflicts." They cite four types of boundary conflicts: compliance, avoidance, controllers, and non-responsives.

Compliance

There are those who are strangled by the noose of compliance. They say "yes" more than they should and to things they should not. They "melt into the demands of other people" who think that they are just wonderful and are often told, "I just don't know what I would ever do without you." The compliant believe it. They fear if they say "no," catastrophe will ensue. No matter how overwhelmed they already are or how unreasonable the request, they just keep saying "yes." The cost is they are under-productive with respect to their own goals, mentally, physically, and spiritually exhausted, financially depleted, and perhaps even bitter. They grieve not being able to get the support they need despite all of the support they give to others. The rope continues to tighten, but they still keep saying "yes."

Avoidance

Next are those who are strangled by the noose of avoidance. They may be highly sought out and viewed as a source of help for others, but it is a one-way street. The avoidant never needs help from others—or at least they are never willing to acknowledge their needs. The compliant struggles with keeping others out. The avoidant struggles with letting others in. The avoidant rationalizes, "I have it," "I can handle it," "I am fine," "It would be easier for me to just figure it out myself." He or she is the superhero—always strong and capable for the sake of others, yet often alone in their own pain.

Controllers

Controllers cannot respect the limits of other people. They may not have much control over their own lives so they take control of the lives of others. Controllers think they know what is best for others so they try to impose their will on them. Rather than seeing the boundaries of others as limits to be respected, they see the boundaries of others as obstacles to overcome. To a controller, "no" may mean "maybe" or "perhaps later" but it does not mean "no."

However, we should not be left with the impression all controllers are aggressive. Some controllers are less direct and abrasive. Some initially come across as "sweet" and even "charming." I've known both a frail elderly woman who shamelessly used her physical illness to manipulate people into doing whatever she wanted, and a strong young man who used his physical advantage to intimidate his girlfriend. Both were controllers.

Non-responsives

Non-responsives don't violate or overstep the needs of others, they simply do not hear them at all. They neglect any emotional responsibility to others, often coming across as "cold" and "insensitive," especially to those closest to them.

According to Cloud and Townsend, in all boundary conflicts "we focus on others and lose clarity about ourselves."

When my niece and nephew were about three and six years old they were into role playing. My nephew decided he was going to role play me. "I'll be Auntie Shannon," he said. When the make believe phone in their make believe house rang, he let out a loud irritated growl. It seemed so ugly and out of place, and I was slightly offended when a dear friend confirmed that had indeed become my typical response. I wasn't doing a good job managing boundaries, and while I hadn't listened to the warnings issued by my chest pains and panic attacks, that six–year-old sure got my attention.

Let's look at the biblical inspiration for our "Dante and Sam story," David and King Saul. This is the quintessential story of a net *becoming* a noose.

> *"David played his harp, as he usually did at such times. Saul had a spear in his hand. Suddenly Saul threw the spear, thinking, "I'll nail David to the wall." David ducked, and the spear missed. This happened twice. Now Saul feared David. It was clear that GOD was with David and had left Saul.*
>
> *So, Saul got David out of his sight by making him an officer in the army. David was in combat frequently. Everything David did turned out well. Yes, GOD was with him. As Saul saw David becoming more successful, he himself grew more fearful. He could see the handwriting on the wall. But everyone else in Israel and Judah loved David. They loved watching him in action.*
>
> *One day Saul said to David, "Here is Merab, my eldest daughter. I want to give her to you as your wife. Be brave and bold for my sake. Fight GOD's battles!" But all the time Saul was thinking, "The Philistines will kill him for me. I won't have to lift a hand against him."*
>
> 1 Samuel 18: 10b-17

The Desire to HELP

Like most toxic entanglements, this one began with the desire to help. It is this desire that first brings David to Saul's attention.

David is a shepherd, and Saul is a king. This seems like an unlikely alliance from the beginning, but when David's eldest brothers serve in Israel's military, David goes back and forth between the military camp and his father's house "trying to help" in both places. At the time it was a cultural and political expectation, so I am not faulting David for helping. But within a person who cannot balance benevolence and self-preservation well, the desire to help can become tragic.

"Compulsive helpers" not only desire to help but also find it difficult to withhold help, and somehow manage to attract the compulsively needy. At first it seems like a good match. On one hand is a person whose self-worth is attached to their being able to fix everything and everyone, and on the other hand is a person who does not have any confidence in their own ability to fix anything. When these two personalities come together it is heaven for both. That is until a net becomes a noose.

I can identify. I am in recovery from being a compulsive helper. I didn't even realize how I was harming myself until I was 28 years old and had been rushed from my doctor's office to the emergency room. I suspected something was wrong when the doctor came into the examination room and watched the nurse re-administer the electrocardiogram (EKG). "We think you may have had a heart attack."

The cardiologist on call in the emergency room wasn't any more comforting. "We have to admit you. I can't risk letting a 28-year-old walk out of here and die of a heart attack." WHAT!

My first cardiology visit was the worst. I was not prepared to be the only one in the waiting room who *didn't* have gray hair. I was not prepared for the doctor to talk to me about factors that were putting me "at risk for a stroke." I was definitely not prepared for the receptionist to hand me orders for six more visits. I sat in my car in the parking lot and cried. Did I mention that I was only 28? I was not prepared! Afterwards, there was a flurry of tests, cardiologists, electrophysiologists, medication, and repeat. I even gave up coffee. Still, my symptoms did not make much sense to me or to the professionals.

Compulsive helpers not only desire to help but also find it difficult to withhold help, and somehow manage to attract the compulsively needy.

That is until one day while I was out having lunch with friends. Just as I was asking them to pray for me regarding this "heart situation," my cell phone rang. The call was brief but changed the whole tenor of the table conversation. As soon as I hung up, one of my friends became very stern. She looked angry, and when I looked to the other friend for some compassionate relief, I didn't find it. Before I could even ask the first friend what was wrong, she said, "I could literally see your heartrate through your neck when you were on that call." She was referring to my carotid pulse, which apparently so intensified she could see it from across the table. "Is that why you are having so many heart problems?" Her next words took my breath away, "We are not going to let her kill you!"

She caught what my cardiologist couldn't catch during a doctor's appointment. The *way* I was loving another friend was killing me. I thought I was just trying to help.

While David is bringing his brothers food at the camp, he hears the taunts of the Philistine champion, Goliath. Goliath was over nine feet tall, wore a bronze helmet, leg armor and javelin, a bronze coat of mail weighing about 125 pounds. He had likely been a warrior his entire adult life. David, who is little more than a boy at this point, is wearing a tunic, some sandals, and carrying a slingshot and some rocks. He is unskilled in battle and has no training. He says, "I'll help!"

Now for those familiar with how the story ends, it is a tale of epic proportions ending with David as a hero and the God of Israel vindicated before the other gods of the world. That is in retrospect. At the time, however, David's action was crazy. Completely irrational. Absolutely nuts!

The desire to help will put us in some precarious situations. Sometimes it will end with the helper as a hero. For those of us

When we invest in helping people who do not define help the way we do, we can end up making substantial investments in their healing while they remain committed to their brokenness.

who are chronic over-helpers, however, our desire to help will cause us to intervene when we should just listen, lead us to act when we should just collect data, and drive us to do for people what they should do for themselves.

Not everyone defines "help" in the same way. *Some* people want to resolve issues, while others want to use the issue to get as much of your time and attention as possible. Both call it "help."

Psychologists refer to the latter as "secondary gain." That is the interpersonal gains or social advantages that come from being troubled in some way. "When I am in distress, everyone rallies to my rescue. I'll keep being irresponsible and ending up distressed, and I have these constant reminders of how much people care for me."

When we invest in helping people who do not define help the way we do, we can end up making substantial investments in their healing while they remain committed to their brokenness. The time, emotional energy, money, and other resources "wasted" can leave us bitter and resolved never to *help* again.

After finding myself on the losing end of "help" time and time again, I developed a help pre-assessment. Asking these transformative questions shifts the mindset of the chronic helper away from "I am the lone hero who must help or else there will be a disaster" and toward "Am I willing and able to be one fiber in the net that supports this person in the situation?"

- Transformative Question 1: What have you already done to address this issue? What has worked? What has not worked?
- Transformative Question 2: To whom have you already spoken/whom have you asked to help with this? What was their response? How are others already engaged in helping?
- Transformative Question 3: Would you like my help with this?
- Transformative Question 4: Specifically, how would you like me to help with this?

If you are not a compulsive helper, this list may seem parochial to you. However, for those of us who are compulsive helpers, when we hear a problem we immediately jump to how we can resolve it and offer a solution before we have these other important pieces of information.

These questions frame the mindset of the helper as well as prime the one receiving help to understand the boundaries of the relationship. Especially in the case in which boundaries have been crossed or blurred previously, an intentional shift is needed.

Think about this for a minute. Imagine a physically healthy man in his late forties. Every morning, he wakes up and gets dressed. He drives to the tallest downtown office building, accesses the janitor's closet, and starts cleaning. He sweeps the stairs and the hallways. Cleans the sinks and the toilets in the bathroom. Takes out the trash in the staff break room, vacuums the offices, washes the windows, and even dusts the furniture. When he notices something is in danger of disrepair, he takes note of it and brings in the appropriate tools to fix it the next day. He does this day after day for weeks. Then one day the "big boss" comes in early and sees him there. The men exchange pleasantries before the "janitor" complains he has not been paid for his work. The boss sincerely apologizes, takes down his name, and promises to speak with the director of human resources as soon as the office officially opens. When the boss brings the matter to the HR director's attention, he is confused to discover that the "janitor" does not work for the company at all. The "janitor" has been working for a company that has not hired him.

Sadly, I have logged many, many hours working for people who did not hire me. Learning to ask the right questions has meant better use of my mental and emotional energies, and more strategic investments of my time and money. I am happier, healthier, less resentful, and definitely more productive.

After you know what type of help is desired, be clear and specific about what help you are willing to give. This means resisting the tendency to see "help" as an all or nothing proposition. We say well-meaning but erroneous things such as, "Whatever you need, I am here." The sentiment is beautiful, but as human beings we have limitations. People experiencing difficulties need a web of support, and the lack of a web might be an important indicator. The one who attempts to be the entire web will find themselves fraying, and maybe even doing harm to the person that they were trying to "help."

David became Saul's entire web, his whole network.

After David confronts Goliath, and miraculously and decisively wins the match over Goliath, Saul would not let him leave. It is not because Saul loves David that he clings to him. It is because he sees something in David he wants for himself. Saul comes to see David as THE answer to his two biggest problems, the near constant threat of war and his personal emotional turmoil. For Saul, David is not a part of the answer, he is the whole answer. "If David is near, I can win battles. If David is near, I can have inner peace."

What an ego boost that must have been for David! He went from being an unknown shepherd to the king's best bud. King Saul sees something of value in him. King Saul wants him to stay close by him. King Saul relies on him. He sees something in David of value, and he "clings" to him. He needs David and wants David near him. Can you imagine the pressure to perform? "The king is dependent on me. The nation is dependent on me! Something about this feels a bit off, but if I don't help, who will?"

They continue on their merry way, and for a while it works. Saul has David near to ensure his own success. David has Saul near to ensure his own significance. Then David starts getting a little too much attention.

One day Saul and David are returning from yet another battle with the Philistines. During the course of the victory parade, Saul hears the song that reveals how he really feels about David. The women in the village begin to sing a song written for the occasion. The lyrics go something like this, "Saul has slain a thousand BUT David has slain ten thousand…Saul has slain a thousand but David ten times more." David doesn't even realize it, but that song is about to change his best bud into his worst enemy.

Here are a few other important questions in evaluating the toxicity of relationship: Am I free to be my full self? Within this relationship, do I have the liberty to celebrate my personal victories and mourn my personal failures? OR do I feel the need to downplay my victories and the impact of my losses because I fear that it will negatively impact the person(s) I am in a relationship with? Can I be as strong as I need to be without worrying about crushing him/her? Can I be as weak as I need to be without worrying about being crushed by him/her? These are vital distinctions.

To be certain Saul was attracted to David because David was strong where he was weak. David could do what Saul could not. Yet David's strength did not eradicate Saul's weakness. While David provided a good cover-up for Saul, the parade song let Saul know the people saw him for who really was. Even, and perhaps *especially* in the presence of David, Saul was still weak.

> *Toxic Relationship Stew*
>
> For the base of this stew, you will need an unagreed upon definition of "help." Once the base comes to a boil, stir in a generous portion of "I am the only one that can help." Sprinkle in 1 cup of either "I am so honored to be asked to help" or "I am obligated to help." Add a generous portion of "inability to refrain from helping." Reduce heat and let simmer until resentment becomes apparent.

It reads like a tried and true recipe.

If an unagreed upon definition of help is one indicator of a toxic relationship, then here is the next…Saul admires and despises David at the same time, and for the same reason. "I love that you are present to help me, but I hate I need your help." This is the pattern keeping David, and so many of us, locked into toxic relationships, praise one moment and punishment the next, and all for the same reason.

What happens next seems like a scene from a *Lifetime* movie. You know, the one in which the charming beau makes a sudden turn into a raving, abusive lunatic? Yes, that one.

Saul has taken his best warrior and makes him his personal minstrel. He can win neither a private battle nor a public battle without him. It is only David's song that gives him peace. Saul *needs* David—and hates him for it.

I imagine as David is providing music therapy for Saul, it suddenly hits Saul "I need this dude too much," and in his anger about his own inadequacy, he lashes out. In a flash of rage, takes a spear and throws it at David. It is likely the same spear that accompanied the two when they marched into war zones together. What was a sign of their camaraderie is now a sign of enmity. What he wants is to "pin David to the wall." He wants to emasculate him, make him unable to move and function effectively. He is not trying to kill him, yet. He wants David near, but he needs David small and limited.

Saul's attack on David is horrific. David risked his life time and time again for Saul. He had been faithful in meeting Saul's needs and available every time he was called on. Of course he didn't have much choice since Saul was, after all, the king, but still David had some choice. With the choice David had, he was faithful. Saul's insecurities have taken center stage, and his action is actually an act of sabotage.

Sabotage is born of insecurity. People who feel they do not deserve their partner may resort to sabotage. People who feel they will not be able to compete on their new job may resort to sabotage. People who fear they will never really be able to lose weight may resort to sabotage. Sabotage is controlled destruction for a sense of restored equilibrium.

When people feel powerless to get the outcomes they want, or to maintain the outcomes they have, they begin to unravel what has been built. It seems counterintuitive to some, but others understand perfectly the thought behind sabotage. "If it is going to burn to the ground, at least I will be in charge of lighting the match." Sabotage!

Consider these examples:

Nicole was dating a man who always told her she was too good for him. At first it was flattering, but it soon became annoying. The relationship was proceeding well otherwise, until he started acting strange. They would make plans, and he would not show up. He wasn't sick, and there were no emergencies. He wasn't being unfaithful. He would just drop out of the relationship from time to time, for no apparent reason at all. After several rounds of this game, Nicole got fed up and ended the relationship. Sabotage!

Jasmine fears she will not be able to handle the demands of her new job. She is older than her colleagues, and her life story is a bit more colorful. She is bright and a hard worker but she is clearly out of her element. She went to community college while raising her child alone. She has always been the big fish in the small pond, but now that she is in the big pond, she doubts she can even swim. Her fear turns to torment when her supervisor pulls her aside to remind her of the office dress code yet again. She doesn't call and doesn't show up to work for a week. She gets let go. Sabotage!

Brad has been told by his doctor he must lose at least fifty pounds, or else he will likely be on medication to control his diabetes for the rest of his life. At 5 feet, 10 inches, and 375 pounds, he has always been a big guy, though not the biggest in his family. In fact, the men in his family wear their size and their eating habits as badges of honor. Brad promises his wife and young children he is going to start eating right and lose the weight and he is really going to stick to it "this time," mainly to stop the flood of tears threatening to burst from his wife's eyes. (She doesn't want to be a young widow like her mother was.) On the way home from a particularly rough day at the office Brad decides to treat himself to a doughnut. He can't decide which flavor he wants so he orders a mixed dozen. "It's cheaper that way, anyway." He promises himself he won't eat them all just before he picks up the fifth one. "But six is an even number...but seven has always been my lucky number...but who has money to waste throwing away five perfectly good donuts." He throws out the empty box before he turns into his neighborhood. Sabotage!

Chapter 9

A Co-Conspiracy

It's quite seductive to see myself as David and to see the people who I tried to help and ended up hurting me as Saul. Me, the kind, compassionate helper, and them, the stark raving lunatic who turned on me. At some point, though, both David and Saul became co-conspirators in the toxic relationship. Even after it became apparent Saul was after David's life, David didn't leave. I can hear the excuses in David's mind, can't you? "Well, he has been going through a tough time lately. He really didn't mean any harm." "It's really a lot of pressure being a king." "Maybe I should have been a little less…or a little more…"

Toxic relationships THRIVE on excusing the inexcusable. One party continues to violate boundaries, while the other party continues to make excuses for them. Sometimes the person in the wrong hasn't even asked to be excused. This lack of relational accountability really damages both parties. When the relationship becomes disproportionately about the needs of one person, freedom and responsibility are not balanced.

Saul made direct attempts against David's life three

times…and David stayed in the relationship with him! This seems crazy, but the truth is, I've done it!

Relational accountability says, "If you want the benefit of being connected to me, you have to honor the boundaries I have set. You don't get to disregard the boundaries and still get the benefits." There are entire psychotherapy modalities developed around this idea of changing the contingencies of relationships, in

When the relationship becomes disproportionately about the needs of one person, freedom and responsibility are not balanced.

order to change problematic and harmful behaviors. The Community Reinforcement Approach to Treatment, for example, is an approach to substance abuse treatment that doesn't directly involve the substance abusers themselves. Instead, therapists work with the affected family members and friends to change their own communication, reinforcement, problem-solving strategies, and self-care. This approach of changing relational contingencies has been effective in getting treatment-resistant substance abusers into treatment.

In relationships we tend to repeat those behaviors that are positively reinforced and diminish or extinguish those behaviors that are not. When we reward people for violating our personal boundaries, what motivation do they ever have to respect those boundaries? Threatened, attempted, and/or actual physical harm of another person is a boundary violation easy to immediately identify. For some, emotional boundary violations are less readily identifiable. However, if we can learn the indicators we can detour much earlier in the road.

David was so busy meeting the needs of Saul he failed to protect himself. When boundaries are not set OR set but not protected, this is not love. Boundaries keep us safe, and when people love each other, they have the utmost concern with the other's safety. Whether it is a romantic partner, family member, coworker, boss, spiritual leader, or friend, if you must always violate your boundaries in order to meet the needs of someone else, you are not in a healthy relationship.

Don't be so busy "helping the Sauls" in your life that you fail to protect yourself.

Chapter 10

Emotional Restructuring of Relationships

Tipping Point

It took quite a while for David to reach his tipping point in his toxic relationship with Saul. Eventually, however, he escapes. He gets out of the relationship. Before we can escape from relationships with a stranglehold on our well-being, we must escape from the exaggerated sense of self-importance. As long as we buy into the assumptions (or even stated beliefs), we alone can save/rescue the other person, the noose will continue to tighten. All the while there is a whispering, "no one else can help them." "I don't want to be like everyone else who abandoned them." "I am all that he has."

We have to begin to examine the assumptions that keep us locked into these toxic relationships. We have to ask the hard questions. Why *hasn't* (s)he been able to maintain other relationships? Can the issue really be with every single person they have ever met, or is the issue with him? What am I getting out of this relationship that is worth my peace? Why do I find it so difficult to prioritize my emotional well-being? Is this a pattern I want to continue to repeat? What am I afraid of? What tie has me in bondage? What truth can set me free?

For some, fleeing from a toxic relationship may actually mean a physical relocation. Quitting an unreasonably demanding job, leaving an abusive partner, dissolving a toxic friendship, blocking an unstable ex on social media and in real life—all are critical elements of flight. However, physical relocation is not always possible or beneficial. For example, when the relationship is with a family member the toxicity can easily ooze across state lines. Whether or not there is a physical relocation, extraction from toxic relationships requires an **emotional restructuring.** That is, the explicit establishment of new boundaries around time, commitments, and emotional availability—and fiercely protecting those new boundaries.

Emotional restructuring of a relationship is HARD—especially the initial conversation. It may seem easier to withdraw or completely drop out of the relationship without any discussion or explanation. Plenty of people choose that route. However, unless there is a concern for personal safety, doing so dishonors the person, your investment, and the relationship itself. Furthermore, it robs both parties of a valuable opportunity to learn and grow. It has been said FEAR can stand for "Forget Everything And Run" or "Face Everything And Rise." It is only by facing our relational problems that we come to have better relationships and better lives.

Prepare for a conversation about the **emotional restructuring** of a relationship by giving some thought to the specific aspects of the relationship that are no longer acceptable to you. (HINT: The vital distinctions discussed in this book can help!) Think about it ahead of time. Also, ahead of time communicate your need for an important conversation and set aside time and space, preferably in person, unless physical safety is a concern. Engaging in some positive self-care in advance of the conversation may help to replenish reserves, reduce tension, and make you more available for the conversation. If possible do something that typically recharges you mentally, emotionally, and/or spiritually. Turn up the volume on your favorite "get hyped" song, spend

Extraction from toxic relationships requires an emotional restructuring.

some extra time in prayer, get a massage, or read something inspiring. Alternatively, you may want to plan something affirming and nourishing for after the conversation.

Remember the relationship cannot be **emotionally restructured** by *planning* the conversation. Neither can the relationship be **emotionally restructured** by *rehearsing* the conversation in your mind. The relationship can only be restructured by resetting the boundaries, and that starts by actually *having* the conversation! Have the conversation. You may be tempted to beat around the bush, to bring up something else, minimize the issues, or to reassure the other person that "everything is all right." Don't. You came to talk about it, so start taking charge of your relationships and your life by having this conversation.

The Difficult Conversation: Step by Step

1. Start with talking about what is good about the relationship, what you value in the person and/or in the relationship that has developed.
2. Give a summative statement about what is no longer acceptable for you. Be prepared with two or three specific examples

illustrating the problem just in case they are needed. Make sure you take responsibility for the things you should take responsibility for—but not for everything.

3. Identify what you are willing to continue to do. Be specific.
4. Identify what you are no longer willing to continue to do. Be specific.
5. Reaffirm your regard for the person. Stick with it!

Some examples:

Emotionally Restructuring in the Workplace

1. *I have been with this company for seven years. I was drawn to its mission and continue to value the work we do. My coworkers are some of the most creative and passionate people that I have ever met, and I have learned a lot here.*
2. *However, over the last eighteen months, my responsibilities have increased significantly. My hours have become longer, resulting in more time away from home, and without any title change or additional compensation.*
3. *While I realize that the company is having financial difficulties, I cannot continue to work 60 hours per week.*
4. *I can commit to working late on Thursday evenings and will prioritize the work detailed in my current job description. Additional assignments can be handled as time permits. While I am open to increased responsibility, I cannot continue to fill multiple roles without a title and salary increase.*
5. *I continue to be committed to this organization and appreciate the opportunity to contribute to its mission.*

Emotionally Restructuring of a Friendship

1. *We have been friends for almost ten years, and I truly*

value our friendship. Your spontaneity and adventurous spirit have challenged me to take more risks in my own life. I really have learned to "enjoy the journey" from you, and I thank you for that.

2. *I know the last eighteen months have been particularly hard for you. I have tried to be a supportive friend, but honestly, I think I have taken on too much. I know things get emotionally intense for you at unexpected times, but being available to talk 24-7 is not sustainable for me.*
3. *I know we both have long commutes, so I would be happy to check in with each other during my evening drive home. I also think it might help if you talked to a professional to help you through this transition. Maybe even one to help you develop a financial plan as well. I would be happy to share my therapist's contact information with you.*
4. *I most definitely want to see you "win," but I will no longer take middle of the night and middle of the work day phone calls. I will also not be able to loan you any more money.*
5. *I love you, I am praying for you and cheering for you. I am confident that you can get through this with the right support team.*

Emotional Restructuring of a Romantic Relationship

1. *We have been dating on and off for almost three years now. When we first met I had lost hope I would ever be able to find someone. Although I was cautious, maybe even overly cautious, your confidence, patience, and sense of humor won me over. We have been able to sup-*

port each other through some hard times, and we have definitely had our share of good times.

2. *But I feel like we are having the exact same arguments now we were having three years ago. Nothing ever gets resolved. We disagree, say hurtful things, break up, and then smooth things over for the sake of "peace." But because we never really resolve the issues, we end up getting back together only to then go through the whole process all over again.*
3. *I will always appreciate all I have learned and the ways that I have grown from this relationship and the good times that we have shared but*
4. *I am not going to do this anymore. I want a relationship in which the needs of both parties are considered, and my needs are not treated as "trivial." I want a relationship in which there is mutual accountability and responsibility. In three years, this has still not become that relationship. Honestly, I have held on longer than I should. But that stops today. Please do not call me anymore. Do not come by my house or reach out to me on social media. I need time and space to heal, and we both know where "just checking on you" usually ends up.*
5. *I really do wish you the best and hope that you find what you need.*

The emotional restructuring of a relationship in no way requires we now hate the other person. My favorite part of the David and Saul story is David keeps his regard for Saul even after he leaves the relationship. Even when Saul became obsessed with harming David, David repeatedly refused to cause harm to Saul. Like the founder of Aikido, who had a goal of creating a martial art that practitioners could use to defend themselves while also protecting their attacker from harm, David decided "It's not you or me, it is you *and* me. I can't be with you, but I can still be for you."

Chapter 11

To Forgive or Not to Forgive, That Is the Question

Mr. C was a family friend and a tenant of my grandparents. As a small child, he seemed generally strange to me—and when he drank, he was kind of scary. He would stand up in the middle of the kitchen floor and start telling these dramatic stories—more like acting them out, really. They were loud, animated, long, and I really couldn't understand all he was saying. Everyone would sit there listening. It was like they knew he needed to tell his story, and even though we had heard the story a million times before, we sat and listened to it. I really had no clue what he was talking about until he got to the shooting parts—there was always a shooting part. When I got a little older, I realized Mr. C had fought in a war and had lived through some horrible times. I suppose his reenactments were his attempts to resolve his experiences in some way.

I suspect most of the people reading this book are not World War II veterans with untreated post-traumatic stress disorder, however, many can identify with Mr. C's strategy. We hold onto painful things. We replay them in our minds, and sometimes reenact them in our current relationships as if by clinging to them we can resolve the hurt. Oddly, the more we cling, the more it hurts us, so we cling more, and it hurts us more. Here is another vital distinction: reenactment versus resolution.

I believe that this is the destructive cycle of clinging to hurts to our detriment is what Jesus was talking about when he taught on the necessity of forgiveness in Luke 17.

One day Jesus said to his disciples, "There will always be temptations to sin, but what sorrow awaits the person who does the tempting! It would be better to be thrown into the sea with a millstone hung around your neck than to cause one of these little ones to fall into sin. So watch yourselves! If another believer sins, rebuke that person; then if there is repentance, forgive. Even if that person wrongs you seven times a day and each time turns again and asks forgiveness, you must forgive." The apostles said to the Lord, "Show us how to increase our faith."

Luke 17:1-5

Sin is the violation of a boundary. When God's boundary has been violated it is called "sin." When man's boundary has been violated it is called "offense." Jesus says while offense is common, inevitable even, the true danger is internalizing the offense. To explain how that works, He uses the illustration of drowning.

Unforgiveness as Drowning?

In the first stage of drowning there is a recognition of danger and a fear response. Perhaps someone has floated out too far and realized their feet no longer touch the bottom of the ocean floor or the pool. Perhaps they get caught in a riptide and realize their normal means of navigating water is not working. Perhaps they have accidentally fallen into deep water and are unable to swim. Whatever the case, something potentially dangerous has happened, and the completely normal response is fear.

Offense almost always has that type of shock value in part because people we have repeatedly experienced as insulting no longer hold the power of surprise over us. We come to them

It is the ones we feel safe who have the greatest power to offend us.

braced. We give ourselves a pep talk before we have to see them and take a deep prayer-filled breath when their name appears on our cell phone screen or in our inbox. We get ourselves ready, because while we may not know *what* they will do, we do know *that* they will do. They can upset us, but rarely offend us.

It is the ones we feel safe with who have the greatest power to offend us. They have passed our tests and have been found "trustworthy." They have our secrets and know our sensitivities. They have tasted our tears—and we theirs. We don't just feel comfortable around them, we feel safe. Struggling to understand each other, difficult but fruitful conversations, exhilarating belly laughs, and knowing glances have granted them access to our souls. Then, without an ounce of warning, we are violently stricken by the poison-soaked arrows of their words or actions. This is offense.

Breathless. We know we *need* to breathe…but in this moment we are not operating at the level of knowing. We are just operating at the level of feeling—and what we want most is to stop feeling. We hold our breaths—not wanting to let anything else that could hurt us while inadvertently keeping out everything that could help us. That's the second stage of drowning—involuntary breath holding.

Once we have been hit with the shock this second stage sets in. "This is too dangerous. I'm not letting anyone or anything else in. I can't!" When we are in emotional danger, we move to protect ourselves. Each of us exhibits varying levels of sophistication with this. The unsophisticated hurl insults and accusations, and maybe even become physically aggressive, which is never, ever acceptable. Then there are those of us who are more nuanced with our breath holding. We can keep the conversation going at a normal tone and pace, offer understanding and acquiescent commentary, or maybe even dismiss the matter altogether by saying, "I understand" or "It's fine." My personal default is, "It doesn't matter." In the time it takes for me to utter those three words, I have taken the offender to court, testified under oath, obtained a ruling in my favor, drawn up the eviction notice, packed up their belongings, and scheduled the moving company to come and evict them from my heart—forever. Except that hearts don't really work like that.

Of course, I'm lying! I am lying to both of us. I know it matters. In fact, it matters so much that I am begging, pleading with myself and with it not to matter quite so much. I am holding my breath, depriving myself of the very truth that I need in order to survive this. That truth is "this hurts unbearably," but I can't say that. That would make me more vulnerable. That would give the other person the opportunity to hurt me even more, and I cannot imagine more pain than this, so in order to protect myself I lie—"I'm fine." I'm trying to help myself, but the pain is... Just. Getting. Worse.

You can only separate yourself from truth for so long before you become unable to discern it. Just as the body deprived of oxygen begins to shut down, so does the soul deprived of truth.

The third stage of drowning is unconsciousness. Emotional responses become more and more narrow, interactions with others become increasingly flat. Bedtime gets earlier and earlier in the evening and lasts later and later into the morning. Perhaps sleep won't come at all. Conversations that used to linger become curt. Whole sentences are exasperating. Simple questions are infuriating.

The good and the bad news about this stage is that while in it you can still go through some of the motions. Sometimes just enough to convince others. Sometimes just enough to convince yourself. Things start to become a bit surreal. Numbness can be a welcomed exchange for pain.

The fourth stage is hypoxic convulsions.

In this fourth stage of physical drowning, movements become erratic. Reactions are illogical. They simply do not make sense given the situation. They are out of sync with the presenting stimuli. I once got cursed out by a stranger I simply smiled at and said hello to. Hypoxic convulsions. People can desperately cling to the very individuals and relationships causing them pain. Hypoxic convulsions. The goal of the behaviors is not clear.

The scariest part is most drowning victims don't yell or wave their arms to alert someone they are in trouble. They are dying—and no one even knows. That's the fifth stage: clinical death.

Unforgiveness wreaks havoc in our lives because it leaves us unable to effectively respond. It leaves us unable to effectively respond to the best in ourselves and in others. It leaves us unable to respond effectively to life's opportunities. It sometimes leaves us unable to effectively respond to God.

Forgiveness is a far cry from the shallow exchange we require of children. We make them say "I'm sorry" to which their injured playmate is expected to say "It's okay" just before they run back onto the playground together. Adults understand that forgiveness is a matter of becoming able to effectively respond to life again. Forgiveness does not mean glossing over it. It is not "just letting it go." That dishonors our pain and leaves us resentful. Forgiveness is not ignoring the discrepancies between my expectations and my reality but confronting them.

We have to figure out what to do with the discrepant information. Do I use it to throw out everything else I know to be true

Forgiveness is a matter of becoming able to effectively respond to life again.

about the person? Will I allow it to totally redefine the relationship? Will I allow it to broaden my perspective on this person? On relationships? On the world? Will I allow this discrepant information to broaden my perspective on myself?

It takes time to know how deeply you have been injured. Therefore, "I will forgive you" may be a more appropriate response to one who has violated our boundaries. By "I will forgive you" we mean "I will not allow this offense to define you completely and forever. Yet, in order to do so I will need to honor my own pain. I will need to explore its contours. I may need to interrogate this pain. I will also need to remember the other parts of you. The parts that bring me joy. At the end of the process I will free both of us from this. I will have relinquished my desire to make you hurt the way that you have hurt me, and I will have relinquished my narrowed perspective of you, but I need the process. I will see you as whole again, and I will be whole again, but in the meantime, this hurts."

I *will* forgive you. Forgiveness is not an event, it is a process.

What's Wrong with Us?

At the time of this writing the news is flooded with images of dead black male bodies murdered by white law enforcement officers, and the acquittal of those officers. Public parks, sidewalks, housing project stairwells, police custody, and routine traffic stops have become the scenes that decry the dark history of racism in the "United" States. The truth is with every new story, I ask myself a question. It is a politically incorrect question and one that could easily offend, but I ask it to myself. "What is wrong with these police?" I suspect I am not the only one who has asked a similar question. As if there were a satisfactory answer or one robust enough to explain the actions of an entire group of people. "What's wrong with white people?" I ask as an African American. "What's wrong with men?" I ask as a woman. "What's wrong with Israelis? What's wrong with Palestinians? What's wrong with Sunni Muslims? What's wrong with Shiites? What's wrong with Democrats? What's wrong with Republicans? What's wrong with poor people? What's wrong with rich people?"

At the heart of all of the politically incorrect questions is the real question...what's wrong with PEOPLE?

I grew up in the northeast, but with southern sensibilities. Both my maternal and paternal grandparents played significant roles in my rearing, and as a result, there were things we just did not do. We did not put feet on furniture. We did not style or play with our hair anywhere near food. We did not lay our bodies or possessions outside on the ground. We did not wear shorts in the winter. We did not go outdoors with wet hair, ever. We did not "talk back" to parents or other elders. We did not refer to people in authority by their first names. The list goes on. When I went away to a predominantly white liberal arts college I met people who did these things all of the time. I was deeply offended. I often thought, "What's wrong with *these* people?"

Isn't it interesting how we so readily identify others as wrong? Don't get me wrong, you will never catch me brushing my hair over coffee, or with a wet ponytail in January, and I still give an occasional side-eye to people who do, but Jesus is helping me. He says in this life, offenses will come. They are inevitable. I mean if you think about it for a moment, the diversity in human experience makes offense impossible to avoid. Everything from being the oldest in the family to being the youngest, being the only child to be being child number six out of twelve, from getting knocked out as a child to getting a time out, from being tall for one's age to being short, being raised in poverty to being raised with wealth, from having a formal education to having street smarts, they all influence our perspective on the world. Our differences influence our perspectives, and our perspectives influence our boundaries.

The vast majority of people do not pathologically put pain to other people. Usually when someone offends us, it is not because they planned to do so. It is usually because the limits of their humanity are rubbing up against the limits of our own.

We assume everyone sees things the way we do, or at least they *should* see things the way we do. I used to wonder why my father would come out of his room holding a dress shirt in one hand and five ties in another to ask, "Which one?" While I could appreciate the fact he wanted his wife and daughters to weigh in on how fashionable he could be for the day, I did not understand the options. At least half of the ties made absolutely no sense given the shirt he was proposing to wear. If he brought out more than one shirt, that made things exponentially worse. Was he trying to be funny? Did he want to embarrass us? Did he have the worst sense of style ever? No, not at all. My father is colorblind. He simply cannot see the distinctions between certain colors like we can. How much time have we spent frustrated or even furious with people who just simply couldn't see the way we do?

With diverse perspectives, experiences, and limits between and among human beings, even ones raised in the same household, how can offense possibly be avoided? According to the Master Teacher, it can't. We will miss the mark with people, and people will miss the mark with us. We will say things that upset others, and others will say things that upset us. We will do things others find offensive, and people will do things that offend us. Offenses will come. Period.

I wonder if we expect too much from people and from ourselves. I recently came across a social media post that stated, "I drop people with no warning. We are getting too old to be explaining to people what they already know they're doing wrong." Wait, WHAT?! I was appalled by how many "likes" and "reposts" this message received. Each of us have a different capacity but all of us have limited capacity. Short-term memory is five plus or minus two items. That is all we can tend to at one time. Usually, those things are the ones most urgent for us. This, of course, is not an excuse to be intentionally offensive, but it is a reason to be gracious to others, and to ourselves when offenses occur. No one will ever be as sensitive to our needs as we are to our own needs—and we will never be as sensitive to the needs of others as they are to their own needs. There are A LOT of things to attend to in life, and A LOT of things to un-attend to in order to survive, such as how your socks feel on your feet or your watch on your wrist. A LOT. And some things will invariably get lost on some of us at the very moment they are found by others. "Dropping" human beings because of an assumption"they know" is not courageous abandonment of immature relationships in pursuit of more promising and fulfilling ones. It is insensitive, cowardly, and frankly hypocritical.

We can be offended without becoming offensive. We can experience hurt without being hurtful. We do not have to drown, just because we have fallen into deep water.

It is a wonder we are not so distracted by the work of daily survival for ourselves and our families we are not permanently offensive to others.

The point I believe that Jesus is making in his teaching on unforgiveness is while it is inevitable that offense will come to us, we can control whether the offense comes through us. We can be offended without becoming offensive. We can experience hurt without being hurtful. We do not have to drown just because we have fallen into deep water.

Differential Impact

While it is true all of us will experience offenses, not all of us will be impacted by it in the same way. Some of us will encounter offense and, despite the shock of it, we will take advantage of the opportunity to examine our own assumptions, deepen our self-exploration, and maybe even broaden our appreciation of others. Offense will actually grow us.

Others of us, however, will encounter offense in a far less productive manner. Rather than examining our own assumptions, we will make assumptions about the motives of the offender. Rather than explore ourselves and interrogate our response to the offense, we will make generalizations about the character of the offender. We will shrink back rather than reach out. We will replay the offense in our minds in ways that reinforce how right we are and how horrible of a person, not simply wrong or different, they are. We will continue to gather evidence against them, with every interaction being a cross-examination to support a verdict that has already been handed down. We won't stop amassing evidence, though. More evidence of their hostility, more evidence of their pettiness, more evidence of their selfishness, more evidence of their ill intent. Any evidence to the contrary will be immediately rejected. We fill ourselves with venom until it is difficult for others to be around us and eventually until it is difficult for us to be with ourselves. Those in this camp will be made bitter. Venom is rarely self-contained. Constantly, each of us must decide, "Which will I be?"

If becoming offended is inevitable but staying offended is detrimental, it would seem that a key to a rich and satisfying life is knowing how to deal with offenses. Having spent fifteen years as a therapist, and thirteen as a pastor, there are few things I have seen do more damage to psychological, physical, and spiritual well-being than offense. I have seen the release of offense cure chronic migraines, lower blood pressure, eliminate digestive problems, resolve cardiac arrhythmias, reverse insomnia, grow hair, brighten skin, and aid in weight loss—and that is just on the individual level. We haven't even scratched the surface of what releasing offense/forgiveness between families, communities, races, and nations could accomplish!

Chapter 12

But How?

People may come to the decision to forgive via many different routes, however, they will all meet at the intersection of "how?" "How do I forgive the person(s) who has injured me?"

A brief psychology lesson is helpful here. According to attribution theory, we tend to explain someone's behavior by attributing a cause to it. Those "causes" are usually either internal or external. Internal causes are ones that are stable and trait-based. External causes are ones that are not stable, but more situational. For example, if Bill asks Matt a question, and Matt responds in a short-tempered manner, according to the attribution theory, Bill will want to understand why Matt responded in that way. Bill's explanation of Matt's short-tempered response will typically run along one of two lines. Either Bill will say to himself something like "Matt is an impatient jerk" or he will say something like "Matt must be hungry."

The first explanation is an internal cause attributing Matt's behavior to a stable, trait-based cause. ("He is a jerk." Yesterday he was a jerk. Today he is a jerk. Tomorrow he will be a jerk. He was probably a jerk as a kid. He will probably die an old man jerk.) The second explanation is an external cause, attributing Matt's behavior to a situational transient cause ("He must be hungry." He does not typically respond this way so there must be a temporary situation that is responsible for his response.)

The fundamental attribution error says when it comes to trying to understand our own *negative* behaviors, we tend to use a situational explanation. "Sorry, I was being short with you. I haven't slept well all week and was really just exhausted." When it comes to explaining our own *positive* behaviors, we lean towards explanations that are more internal. "Of course I won the game, I am brilliant!"

The exact opposite is true, however, when we try to explain the behaviors of others. In explaining the behaviors of others, we tend to assume their *negative* behaviors are the result of stable traits ("He is an insensitive jerk") and their *positive* behaviors are the result of situational conditions ("She got lucky today").

Attribution theory makes a significant contribution to our understanding of forgiveness. Specifically, it helps us to understand why it is so difficult to forgive, and it provides a key to our entering the process.

In the Tyler Perry movie *Why Did I Get Married?* two women approach their mutual friend concerning their marital problems. Both women are struggling with being vulnerable in their marriage. When the two women approach their friend, a psychologist whose own marriage suffers after the loss of a child, she gives them each a piece of paper and this advice: "On one side of the paper, write down all of the good things that he has done for you. On the other side, write down all of the bad. If the bad outweighs the good, then there is no need to hold on. But if the good outweighs the bad, then fight for your marriage."

The simple exercise helps the women overcome the "error" in their fundamental attributions—the tendency to see their husbands' negative or undesirable behavior as a stable trait rather than as situational. It is also intended to help the women look at their own stable traits that are negatively impacting the situation—in this case their lack of vulnerability. I suspect many people who have watched this movie tried this "make a list" approach. I'd like to offer some additional tools for your "pursuing forgiveness tool kit" because if you decide to forgive, you will want to know how.

Attempts to build consensus around our offense can quickly turn into building more offense.

I want to offer three ways in which you can balance your attributions of others, and thereby forgive. These include giving attention to the following: conversation, observation, and rumination.

Forgiveness through Conversation

The desire to have others affirm our pain is understandable and even normal. The shock of offense may leave us disoriented and doubting our own data collecting ability, therefore even more desirous of an outsider's perspective. "He said_____. That's crazy, right?" It is the emotional equivalent of showing a loved one a cut or a bruise. While they may not be able to resolve it, the acknowledgment certainly helps. However, such attempts to build consensus around our offense can quickly turn into building more offense. There may be people in your circle eager to validate the offense, but less eager to encourage the forgiveness. It may be good policy to share offenses only with people who have a track record of being merciful and themselves forgiving. They are the ones most likely to hear your pain in a focused and compassionate way, and also to help you pan out to see the bigger picture. They are the ones who lovingly help you overcome your faulty attributions rather than build on them.

If you do not have a person like that in your life, God works! "Pray for your enemies."

Once you have made the decision to forgive intellectually, changing your conversation about the person who offended you will help uphold your decision. You won't feel like it, but if the current way you are talking about it is making you angrier, sadder, and more bitter, something needs to change. Emotions have a way of catching up to words. Shifting the conversation from pain caused, blame assigned, and fault found toward resolution possible, understanding sought, and treasure hunted is an essential part of the forgiveness process. Gracious conversation conditions our hearts towards gracious action.

Forgiveness through Observation

Have you ever noticed when a friend gets a new car you start seeing that same make and model of car everywhere? Suddenly the whole world is driving a Honda Pilot just because your friend brought one. Here's the point: What we give attention to magnifies. We tend to observe more of what we have observed. A second component of forgiveness is observation.

In short, what we look for we will find. If we have decided

someone is dishonest, arrogant, rude, or untrustworthy we will certainly find evidence of it. Whether relationships or police investigations, we can find evidence to prove our initial, and potentially biased, theory. However, when we operate in this mode, even ambiguous actions are perceived as offensive.

I grew up watching the sitcoms of the '70s and '80s. A very popular plot line centered around misunderstanding or miscommunication. In the opening scene of each episode, there would be a critical misunderstanding or a miscommunication that left one character offended. For several subsequent scenes the offender would go about his or her business, completely oblivious of the offense their action has caused. Meanwhile the offended party's distress would gradually heighten, and totally neutral actions would be interpreted as insulting or threatening until there was finally a culminating encounter in which the original misunderstanding was uncovered and the subsequent misunderstandings and tensions collapsed like a house of cards. The writers of *What's Happening* and *Three's Company* were masterful at this! Everyone kisses and makes up, they affirm the importance of what was almost lost, the credits roll, the studio audience applauds, the television audience breathes a sigh of relief, and they do it all again the following week.

Psychologists refer to the tendency to look for information that confirms what we already believe about a person or a situation as "confirmation bias." ("He is so selfish. Yesterday he forgot my birthday, and today he is hogging the TV remote.") We interpret new data in light of existing beliefs and even selectively remember details confirming what we believe while ignoring details disconfirming what we believe. The problem is that, as with any bias, confirmation bias leads us to exclude information critical to making a truly informed and effective decision.

When we decide to forgive someone with whom we are still angry or offended, what is least easy for us to do is also the most beneficial and necessary. That is, we must search for disconfirming evidence.

Attempts to build consensus around our offense can quickly turn into building more offense.

We will naturally be drawn to information confirming our right to be angry, however, one of the ways we advance in the process of forgiving is to look for information that disproves my theory. What evidence is there this person is trustworthy? That they are concerned about my best interest? That they do care about me? Disconfirming observations help us to move from "fault finding" to "treasure hunting."

I imagine at this point someone deep in the throes of betrayal will say, "Wait a minute, I am not going to let them back in. The pain is just too deep and I cannot risk that again, no matter what anyone says!" To that person I say, don't worry. What we are talking about now is forgiveness, not reconciliation. The commitment to forgive and the commitment to reconcile are two entirely different decisions, and they should be. We will turn our attention to the relationship between forgiveness and reconciliation shortly, but first, one more tool in our forgiveness tool kit.

Forgiveness through Rumination

When we have been offended we want to understand. "Why

did this happen?" "What did I do to deserve this?" "Where did this come from?" "How could I have missed that?" "What does this change?" That is normal. Normal, normal, normal. Asking questions like these can be helpful. While at some point most of us have heard, "There is no such thing as a dumb question," I would argue not all questions, and not all questioning, are created equal.

Questioning that leads to problem solving, deeper understanding, and results in forward movement is good! Questioning that increases feelings of helplessness, anxious uncertainty, and results in emotional paralysis is not good!

Faith fuels forgiveness.

We get our term "ruminate" from the digestive process of cattle, sheep, goats, buffalo, deer, elk, giraffes, and camels, collectively known as ruminants. These animals have four components to their stomachs and have the ability to "voluntarily vomit." This ability allows them to bring up previously swallowed food in order to break it down further for better digestion and absorption of nutrients. Sounds gross, right?

When we speak of psychological rumination we typically refer to thinking about the same things over and over and over. That process is not bad if, like cows, we are absorbing more nutrients. If we are replaying a scene, conversation, or incident over and over in our minds and rather than broadening and becoming mobilized, we are narrowing and becoming paralyzed, it is a problem. Unable to leave that place of offense in our minds, we hold our offenders hostage to the offense, and we hold ourselves hostage to its pain.

By obsessively replaying, rehearsing, and reenacting we are re-injuring ourselves. With the pain so fresh, forgiveness will be all the more difficult.

Have you ever heard someone recount a painful incident with such vivid detail and emotional intensity you thought it just occurred yesterday? I have! I was shocked to discover the relational injury they were sharing happened years earlier. It was alive, present, and causing intense pain because it was being constantly fed in the mind of the offended person. STOP IT! Take a break. Call a timeout. Detach. You can make an appointment to come back to it later. Don't entertain it again before that scheduled appointment. Put your mouth on something else (conversation). Put your eyes on something else (observation). Put your mind on something else (rumination). This offense has already taken up enough of you!

At the Heart of Forgiveness

We hold onto our grudges and offense as a means of protecting ourselves from more pain. It makes sense, until we realize how holding on actually causes more pain. We will be touched by things we would have never chosen. Heartache, betrayal, disappointment, and traumatic loss are not chapters any of us would include in our life's story. They may shake us to the core and leave us doubting our identity and purpose. We can, however, realize all is not lost and it may not be up to me to reclaim what is. Ultimately, forgiveness is a matter of faith.

It is not a fluke that after Jesus talked to His disciples about the power of forgiveness, one of them responds, "Increase our faith." It is faith that fuels our ability to expel rather than absorb offense. Faith in who we are, faith in the good purposes unfolding in our lives, and faith in God make the work of forgiveness possible. Faith says, "This person has violated a boundary that you set, but your boundaries are still important." Faith says, "This did not work out the way you thought it would, but there is still good ahead of you." Faith says, "This has been almost unbearable, but God will help you get through it." Faith says, "There is still opportunity in the world, you can let go of this one and try again."

One of the reasons boundary violations that occur in childhood are so challenging to resolve (although not impossible) is because children are in the very early stages of developing faith. Faith fuels forgiveness.

Chapter 13

Are There Limits on Forgiveable?

In April 2014, *The New York Times* published an article about reconciliation among Rwanda's Hutu and Tutsi.

"He killed my father and three brothers. He did these killings with other people, but he came alone to me and asked for pardon. He and a group of other offenders who had been in prison helped me build a house with a covered roof. I was afraid of him—now I have granted him pardon things have become normal, and in my mind I feel clear."

Viviane Nyiramana, survivor

"I used to hate him. When he came to my house and knelt down before me and asked for forgiveness, I was moved by his sincerity. Now, if I cry for help, he comes to rescue me. When I face any issue, I call him."

Evasta Mukanyandwi, survivor

"Many among us had experienced the evils of war many

times, and I was asking myself what I was created for. The internal voice used to tell me, 'It is not fair to avenge your beloved one.' It took time, but in the end we realized that we are all Rwandans. The genocide was due to bad governance that set neighbors, brothers and sisters against one another. Now you accept and you forgive. The person you have forgiven becomes a good neighbor. One feels peaceful and thinks well of the future."

Cesarie Mukabutera, survivor

If ever there were a group of people whose unforgiveness would be justified, it would be these women. During the 100 days of the Rwandan genocide as many as one million Tutsis and moderate Hutus (seen as Tutsi sympathizers) were slaughtered. Neighbors took up machetes against neighbors. At the behest of government and the military, friends turned against each other, communities were looted, homes destroyed, and families ripped apart. Rape was used as a weapon of war. As if the genocide were not horrific enough, the inactivity of the world community, including the United Nations and the United States, fueled the fire. This was one of the most appalling mass human rights violations of my lifetime, and a truly dark moment for humankind. Most of us watched it on the news, but these women lived it. It is what they survived, and what they choose to forgive.

They decided not to let the injury caused be the defining factor of their perpetrators. They would come to see them as whole humans, humans who had done horrific things, but whole humans nonetheless.

Then they took a giant leap: reconciliation. That is our final vital distinction: forgiveness versus reconciliation.

Forgiveness says, "I will restore your place in my heart." I will do the work necessary to see you as a whole again: my fellow human being whom I had no reason to fear, the husband I have loved for all of these years, the mentor I have come to respect and appreciate, the family member I could rely on, the friend I had come to trust. I will do that work.

But reconciliation is different. Reconciliation says, "I will actually give you that place back in my life." Forgiveness means we restore the value of a person in our heart, but reconciliation means we restore their position in our life. It is the difference between admiring something online and actually purchasing it.

Here is why this matters. If we forgive without reconciling we can be throwing away people who can otherwise bring significant value to our lives. We also can be robbing ourselves of the opportunity to grow and mature emotionally. If we reconcile without forgiving we allow someone close to us again, to make it more convenient to cause us pain.

Consider the example of a man who has been unfaithful to

Forgiveness means we restore the value of a person in our heart, but reconciliation means we restore their position in our life.

his wife. She can't stand the sight of him. She hates him bitterly and "has every right to." She doesn't care if he sleeps on the street, he will never return to the home. She files for a divorce, thinking she will be done with him forever and move on with her life. It is years before she realizes how her bitterness toward her husband harmed their children and has caused her to push away other men who have expressed interest in her since their divorce.

She wonders if it is even why she has aged so much, has had so many ulcers, or if it is why her previously promising career has stalled. Unforgiveness is drowning.

Or perhaps they have an explosive argument and she puts him out of the house, but after a couple of days the expense of him staying in a hotel becomes prohibitive so he returns "home." Although she hasn't decided whether she wants to forgive him and "try to work things out," they resume marital business as usual. Except now their interactions are angry and destructive. He saw the return home as a promising sign, but since he has returned, the only place he wants to be is somewhere else. It seems everything comes back to the affair, and while he realizes how wrong he was, he wonders if she really will punish him forever. Reconciliation without forgiveness.

Or they decide they "are determined to make things work." It will be a long road, but he understands they both need to fully honor her pain, as well as his. It will mean a lot of hard conversations. It will mean "starting over" in some ways. It will mean calling to check in a lot more often, sharing all of his passwords, and spending a lot less time hanging out "with the boys." It will mean sometimes she may be distant, and he will check in to be reassured she is not done with the relationship, but she is doing the ongoing work of processing. He will need to be consistent in order to, over time, regain her trust. She will need to be willing to acknowledge his efforts in order to restore his value in her heart. They do the work of forgiveness and reconciliation and discover they are stronger as individuals and as a team than they ever imagined they would be.

Or they just cannot get past it. She discovers it was not an isolated event, but a pattern over many years, and every time she had suspicions, she was correct. They give it a sincere effort, but the more they try, the more they seem to hurt each other. The more they talk, the more deceptions they discover. Self-deceptions and deceptions of the other become quicksand. They are not sure whether they will make it as partners, but each knows the other is an amazing parent. They decide no matter what happens with their marriage, they will work together to co-parent their children. Forgiveness without reconciliation.

People will occasionally violate our boundaries. Offense will come. Usually these violations are not due to malice but to mis-calculation. Trustworthy people, those with whom reconciliation is a possibility, are those who quickly learn from their miscalculations. Untrustworthy people are those who do not.

Chapter 14

A Higher Ethic Still: Living by Mercy

"The day I thought of asking pardon I felt unburdened and relieved. I had lost my humanity because of the crime I committed, but now I am like any human being."

Dominique Ndahimana, perpetrator, Rwandan genocide

What is mercy? It has been spoken about in many ways, but I find its most satisfying definitions to be biblical ones, primarily because biblically, mercy is never simply effective. Biblically speaking, mercy is not merely a feeling, but a disposition giving rise to action, and if an action does not contain both position of heart and positive action, it is not mercy. Mercy is an intentionally cultivated inner quality that always shows up somewhere.

Mercy is not simply feeling bad someone is suffering, it is the removal of misery, compassionate attentiveness, unsolicited comfort, and kindness to the least expectant and least "deserving."

Mercy is not to merely notice impending danger, it is to rescue those in actual danger and provide help to those at risk of danger. It is the relief of burden and the restoration of lost fortunes. Mercy is the forfeiture of privilege in the service of the disenfranchised. It is withholding power to harm and extending power to aid. Mercy is gracious acquittal.

It can be easier to think about what mercy looks like under particular conditions. "What does mercy look like when I pull up to the intersection and the homeless beggar approaches?" But

Mercy is not simply feeling bad someone is suffering, it is the removal of misery, compassionate attentiveness, unsolicited comfort, and kindness to the least expectant and least "deserving."

what of mercy as a rule of life? What if mercy was not what we did when we came upon some suffering, but a lens through which we approached all of life? Or a rhythm to which every other action or non-action must be syncopated? Could we really think mercy, live mercy, eat mercy, shop mercy, drive mercy, spend mercy, schedule mercy, and speak mercy?

Could you imagine a community in which the cultural ethos was simply mercy? "Mercyville?" What would intimate relationships look like? In such a place "family" couldn't possibly be limited to those with shared DNA, could it? Would there even be a word in the language for "orphans" or "illegal immigrant" or "homeless" or "poor?" What would it mean for business relationships? What about government, law enforcement, social services, health, business, finance, mental health, and education reform? Would these even exist? Might the distinctions we use to navigate our matrix of social and political relationships prove archaic? Would the truly free people of this land just provide what is needed for their neighbor to flourish because they understand that their own flourishing is intertwined? It sounds almost utopian, doesn't it? I wonder.

References

Cloud, Henry, and John Townsend. *Boundaries: When to Say Yes, How to Say No to Take Control of Your Life.* Harpercollins Christian Pub, 2017.

"Drowning Prevention." *Https://Phpa.health.maryland.gov.*pdf

Frankl, Viktor. *Man's Search for Meaning.* Beacon Press, 2006.

Holy Bible: New Living Translation. Tyndale House Publishers, 2013.

hooks, bell. *All about Love: New Visions.* Harper Perennial, 2016.

Hugo, Pieter. "Portraits of Reconciliation." *The New York Times,* 4 Apr. 2014, www.nytimes.com/interactive/2014/04/06/magazine/06-pieter-hugo-rwanda-portraits.html.

Lama, Dalai, and Tutu, Desmond. *Book of Joy.* Arrow Books Ltd., 2018.

Love It or List It. HGTV.

Mason, Shannon. "Using Qualitative Research Methodology to Explore How Recovering Substance Abusers Utilize Religion to Facilitate Substance Abuse Recovery." *Temple University,* 2006.

Stockwell, John. *Crazy/Beautiful.* 2001

About the Author

As a counseling psychologist, pastor and organizational strategist, Dr. Shannon Mason has one aim, to connect individuals and organizations to their created purpose. Her passion is the development of strategies to help optimize gifts, and she has spent the last twenty years doing just that.

Over the past twenty years she has held a variety of positions that have fed her passion for growth including as a non-profit executive director, health messaging and substance abuse researcher, adjunct professor, clinician, and family support worker. As a mission strategist her work now focuses primarily on strengthening core skills needed to navigate organizational transition.

She is a senior pastor of New and Living Way Ministries, a church she planted in September 2004.

Dr. Shannon Mason holds a Bachelors' Degree in Psychology from Trenton State College, a Master's Degree in Psychological Services from the University of Pennsylvania, and a Doctor of Philosophy Degree in Counseling Psychology from Temple University. She served for eight years as the director of children and youth services initiatives for a large community-based human services organization in Trenton, New Jersey. She also served as Executive Director of Mercer Street Friends, overseeing programs, administrative and fiscal operations, and developing initiatives for the anti-poverty organization which serves 30,000 Mercer County residents annually.

A Note from the Author

A review is the most valuable gift you can give an author. Honest reviews are an invaluable tool for authors, helping them to become recognized for their work and helping them to connect with readers who are looking for new authors and interesting new books to read. If you enjoyed this book, I would whole-heartedly appreciate it if you'd take the time to leave a review when you reach the review link at the end of this book. If you do write one, please send me an email at shannonmasonllc@gmail.com so I can thank you personally.

Made in the USA
Columbia, SC
22 September 2019